COMPLETE

# On the BEATEN PATH
# BEGINNING DRUMSET COURSE
An Inspiring Method to Playing the Drums. Guided by the Legends

## RICH LACKOWSKI

D1710010

## CONTENTS

Charlotte Community Library
Charlotte MI 48813

Alfred Music Publishing Co., Inc.
P.O. Box 10003
Van Nuys, CA 91410-0003
alfred.com

Copyright © MMXII by Alfred Music Publishing Co., Inc.
All rights reserved. Printed in USA.

No part of this book shall be reproduced, arranged, adapted, recorded, publicly performed, stored in a retrieval system,
or transmitted by any means without written permission from the publisher. In order to comply with copyright laws, please apply for
such written permission and/or license by contacting the publisher at alfred.com/permissions.

ISBN-10: 0-7390-8099-7 (Book & DVD)
ISBN-13: 978-0-7390-8099-3 (Book & DVD)

Cover photos: Drumsets © Larry Lytle • Drumset provided courtesy of DW/PDP • Drummer on hwy: © iStockphoto.com/Anja Peternelj •
Highway: © iStockphoto.com/P.Wei • Live band: © iStockphoto.com/Shawn Gearhart • Green arrow sign: © iStockphoto.com/Juan David Ferrando •
Drummer in silhouette: © iStockphoto.com/Dan Van Oss • Blurry kit with red light: © Alamy

Other photos: Photos Page 5 © Laurel Geare · Steven Adler © Neil Zlozower · John Bonham © Robert Knight · Tré Cool © Getty Images / Ethan Miller ·
Steve Gorman © Marty Temme · Dave Grohl © Marty Temme · Levon Helm © Leo Kulinsky Jr. · Phil Jones © Jimmy Callian ·
Joey Kramer © Getty Images / Kevin Mazur · Ian Paice © Marty Temme ·Phil Rudd © Getty Images /Michael Ochs ·
Alex Van Halen © Getty Images / Paul Natkin · Meg White © Getty Images / Stephen Lovekin · Art Blakey © Time & Life Pictures/Getty Images / Robert Parent ·
Jeff Hamilton © Redferns / Clayton Call · Al Jackson, Jr. © Getty Images / Michael Ochs · Philly Joe Jones © Getty Images / Robert Abbott Sengstacke ·
Steve Jordan © Redferns / Clayton Call · Chris Layton © Redferns / Clayton Call · Mitch Mitchell © Getty Images / Michael Orchs ·
Buddy Rich © Lissa Wales / www.drumpics.com · Max Roach © Lee Tanner/The Jazz Image · Ringo Starr © T. Eagan ·
Vinnie Colaiuta Courtesy of The Avedis Zildjian Company, Inc. · Sly Dubnar © Wonder Knack · Jon Fishman © Phish/Danny Clinch ·
Zigaboo Modeliste Courtesy of Vic Firth, Inc. · Neil Peart © Andrew MacNaughtan · Jabo Starks Courtesy of Vic Firth, Inc. · Lars Ulrich © Neil Zlozower

Alfred Cares. Contents printed on 100% recycled paper.

**This book is designed** to help you get "on the beaten path," that is, to help you play the beats and solos that our mighty drumming forefathers play on the songs we love. You will learn everything you need to know to go from the first thought of "I want to play the drums" to playing some of the most legendary beats and solos ever recorded! Many books claim to do this very thing, but what sets this book apart from the rest is that here, you will learn by playing along with the greatest drummers in the world—all types of famous drummers from a variety of musical styles—and you'll learn how to play the beats that they perform on some of the most famous songs ever recorded. This book explains what these drummers play on their songs by breaking it down in a way that gets you to learn to read music and start developing your own ideas into beats, fills, and solos.

I believe that drummers learn by mimicking their heroes. Sure, beats grow and change and morph into original ideas, but all drummers—from aspiring beginners to seasoned professionals—are naturally inspired by what other drummers are playing. The proof is in all those people you've seen air drumming along to some key part in a song. Many of these people have never sat behind a drumset or even held a drumstick, but the drum beat and the framework of the song somehow gets them to raise their arms in the air and act out their interpretation of a moving drum passage. It's

basic human instinct. When writing this book, I wanted to guide this natural instinct in a way that logically feeds you information as you need it so you can accelerate the process of learning how to play your drumming heroes' beats.

I know when I first started playing the drums, even though I had just begun taking group lessons on the snare drum in school, that the *real* learning happened when I got home and threw down my boring class snare drum book that our teacher assigned to us. I put on the headphones each day, sat behind my drum kit, and tried to mimic the beats and fills that the drummers were playing on my favorite songs. Through trial and error, I was eventually able to play the songs and at least fake my way through the more difficult parts.

In this book, I will accelerate this process of trial and error, and guide you through the things that every drummer needs to know in order to play the drums. This book can be used with or without a teacher. Although you don't *need* a teacher to use this book, it would benefit you to go find a drum teacher in your area and take lessons. A teacher will get you to practice if nothing else, but they will also correct any bad techniques you may be developing before they become hard-to-break habits.

Now let's get started and begin our journey On the Beaten Path!

## Icons Used in This Book

The following icons are used throughout this book to help you learn valuable information and to become a better drummer.

 **TIP:** This icon is shown near helpful tidbits of advice.

 **TOOL:** This icon is shown near key concepts or tools that will help you play the drums with more expression and personality.

 **TERM:** This icon is shown near explanations of key music notations and concepts.

# CONTENTS

786.
919
L

4

*Audio examples performed by Rich Lackowski.*
*Instructional photos by Larry Lytle.*

**Rich Lackowski** is the author of the award-winning series of On the Beaten Path music instruction books. The first book in the series, *On the Beaten Path: The Drummer's Guide to Musical Styles and the Legends Who Defined Them* (Alfred Music Publishing, 2007) was highly acclaimed by teachers, students, and drumming enthusiasts alike, and has earned Lackowski accolades from around the world. The book was voted "No. 1 Educational Book" in *Modern Drummer's* 2008 Reader's Poll, and voted "No. 1 Book" in *DRUM!* magazine's 2008 Reader's Poll. *Drumscene* magazine (Australia) called it the "future groove and reference bible for a huge part of the modern drumset." Drummerworld.com (Switzerland) called it "the best book I've seen—a masterpiece." MikeDolbear.com (UK) called it "a must for any serious drummer." *Drumheads!! Schlagzeugmagazin* (Germany) called it "An extraordinary book." *Percussioni* magazine (Italy) called it "a great method for students who want to teach themselves, and for teachers looking for materials to help them expose students to a variety of drumming styles." Bob Gatzen (USA), a highly respected teacher, author and inventor, called it "a major breakthrough for drumset method books" and went on to say "no doubt, you're re-inventing the standard."

The success of the book prompted Lackowski to author his next two books, *On the Beaten Path: Progressive Rock* (Alfred Music Publishing, 2008) and *On the Beaten Path: Metal* (Alfred Music Publishing, 2009), expanding his best-selling book into a series that further addressed drummers' interests. Both books have been well received by the drumming community and have received praise similar to that of the pioneer book. In fact, *On the Beaten Path: Progressive Rock* was voted as one of the "Top 2 Educational Books" in *Modern Drummer's* 2009 Reader's Poll and was voted among the "Top 3 Educational Books" in *DRUM!* magazine's 2009 Reader's Poll. *On the Beaten Path: Metal* was voted among the "Top 4 Educational Books" in *DRUM!* magazine's 2010 Reader's Poll.

The global success of the series spawned a translation of Lackowski's original book *On the Beaten Path* into German and was released in Europe under the title *Drum Masterclass* (Alfred Publishing Verlags GmbH, 2009). Italian translations for *On the Beaten Path* and *On the Beaten Path: Metal* were also released in 2009 and 2010 respectively (Volontè & Co).

Lackowski is also a clinician, teaching drum workshops at music stores around the world and at prestigious events including Australia's Ultimate Drummer's Weekend in Melbourne, Australia in 2010.

In addition to authoring the On the Beaten Path series of successful music instruction books, Lackowski is an endorsed artist and member of the Vic Firth Education Team, an endorsed artist with Evans Drumheads and member of the D'Addario Educational Committee, he's written articles and features for *TRAPS* magazine and *How to Play Drums* magazine, and he's performed in various locations around the world since 1985.

Lackowski was born and raised in Chicago, Illinois, lived in West Lafayette, Indiana, and Detroit, Michigan, until he moved to Los Angeles, California, where he has resided since 2001. He's played the drums since age 10 and is currently playing drums in the Nikki O'Neill Band.

Several individual components make up a complete drumset. These components can be grouped into three major categories—drums, cymbals, and hardware—each of which are described below.

## Drums

1. **Kick Drum:** Also called a bass drum, this is the largest-sized and lowest-pitched drum in the kit. It rests on its shell on the floor, and it's played by pressing your foot on a kick pedal that swings a mallet to strike the drumhead. The kick drum is typically 18–26 inches in diameter, with the most common size being 22 inches.

2. **Snare Drum:** This drum and the kick drum are the most-used drums in the kit. Characterized by metal snares that are pressed against the bottom head, the snare drum is usually 14 inches in diameter with a shell made from either wood or metal.

3. **Rack Toms:** These drums are usually mounted above the kick drum and typically vary in size from 8–15 inches, with the most common sizes being between 10 and 13 inches.

4. **Floor Tom:** This is similar to a rack tom, but is larger in size, supported by three legs attached to the drum, and typically positioned on the right side of the drumset. Floor toms typically range in size from 14–18 inches, with the most common size being 16 inches.

## Cymbals

5. **Hi-Hats:** Positioned horizontally to the floor, these two cymbals are mounted on a hi-hat stand, one on top of the other so the cymbal bells face away from each other. Hi-hat cymbals typically range in size from 13–15 inches, with 14 inches being the most commonly used size.

6. **Crash:** These cymbals typically range in size from 13–20 inches, with 16–18 inches being the most commonly played sizes. Small crash cymbals are often called splash cymbals, and usually range in size from 6–12 inches.

7. **Ride:** This cymbal is usually larger and heavier than a crash cymbal and produces a "ping" sound that's more defined and focused than the big, explosive, washy "wave-crashing" sound of the crash cymbals. Ride cymbals typically range in size from 18–24 inches and are most commonly 20–22 inches.

## Hardware

8. **Cymbal Stands:** These are used to support the crash, splash, and ride cymbals.

9. **Snare Stand:** This stand supports the snare drum.

10. **Hi-Hat Stand:** This stand is used to support the hi-hat cymbals and has a foot pedal assembly that clamps the hi-hat cymbals together when pressed down.

**11. Hi-Hat Clutch:** This special mounting bracket keeps the top hi-hat cymbal mounted to the top of the hi-hat stand.

**12. Kick Pedal:** The kick pedal is mounted to the kick drum and is operated by the foot. When pressed down, the kick drum beater strikes the kick drum head.

**13. Throne:** This is the drummer's seat.

# This section describes commonly accepted ways of positioning the drums to your body.

The overall idea when setting up your drums is to make sure you can strike each drum and cymbal comfortably and easily. You shouldn't have to lean or stretch uncomfortably to hit anything.

Set up your drums on a drum rug. This will help keep any grease from your pedals off of your floors and nice carpets, and will also keep your drums from sliding all over the place. Any basic remnant from a carpet store will do—look for denser styles rather than plush or shag carpeting.

**Throne:** Adjust the seat height so that your thighs are parallel to the floor, or sloping downward at a slight angle, when your feet are on the kick and hi-hat pedals. Move the throne forwards, towards the kick drum, or backwards, away from the kick drum, so your heel is directly below, or just slightlyforward of, your knee. You're in the proper position when your lower leg is just about perpendicular to the floor, and your lower leg and upper leg form an approximately 90-degree angle.

**Kick Drum:** Position the kick drum so it is perpendicular to your right leg. Your foot should rest comfortably on the footboard of the kick pedal. You may have to move the kick drum closer to you or away from you until your lower leg is perpendicular to the floor.

**Snare Drum:** The snare drum should be positioned directly between your legs so that you can easily and comfortably strike the drum with either hand. To get the proper snare drum height, follow these steps. Sit on the throne and let your arms hang freely straight down by your sides. Maintain this upper arm position while raising your forearms until they are parallel cwith the floor. Make sure your palms are facing down towards the floor when you move into this position. Raise or lower your snare drum stand so the top of the snare drum is a few inches lower than your forearms when they are in this position. Set the angle of the snare drum stand so the drum is parallel to the floor, or tilted just slightly towards you.

**Hi-Hat:** Position the hi-hat so your left foot comfortably rests on the footboard while your lower leg is perpendicular to the floor. Adjust the height of the cymbals so that they are 8–16 inches above the snare drum when closed. Adjust the hi-hat clutch so that the cymbals are roughly ½–1 inch apart when opened. If the cymbals are exactly parallel to each other, they will act like suction cups and will stick to each other when you step on the hi-hat pedal. To avoid this, adjust the bottom hi-hat cymbal tilter mechanism so the bottom cymbal is slightly angled.

**Rack Toms:** Position the rack toms directly above the kick drum, angled slightly towards you, and angled slightly in towards each other. The toms should be positioned about an inch away from each other. Make sure they are high enough so that they aren't scraping against your kick drum, but not so high that you can't hit them.

**Floor Tom:** Position the floor tom on your right side at a height roughly equal to the snare drum, and angled slightly towards you.

**Cymbals:** Position each cymbal so that you can easily crash their edges and also play their tops and bells. The bell of a cymbal is the bowl-shaped part that raises up in the center towards the hole. Crash cymbals are generally mounted above the rack toms around eye-level height, spread out a bit wider than the toms, and angled slightly towards you. The ride cymbal is generally mounted on the right side of the kit, above the floor tom, and is angled and set back a bit so that you can comfortably play the half of the cymbal that's closest to you and the bell of the cymbal.

**In this section, we'll learn how to use the matched (German) grip.** This is the most common "modern" grip used by countless drummers, including Meg White (The White Stripes), John Bonham (Led Zeppelin), Joey Kramer (Aerosmith), Dave Grohl (Nirvana), and Tré Cool (Green Day), just to name a few.

**❶** Sit on the throne and let your arms hang freely straight down by your sides.

**❷** Maintain this upper arm position while raising your forearms until they are parallel with the floor. Make sure your palms are facing down towards the floor when you move into this position.

**❸** Now, loosely hold the drumsticks so that the forward two-thirds of each drumstick is showing. You want to grip the stick between your thumb and the first joint of your index finger. (The first joint is the first crease closest to your fingertip.)

**4** Lightly close your remaining fingers so that they just touch the drumstick. Make sure you're still gripping the sticks loosely and that your palms are still facing down towards the floor.

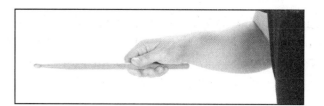

If you start developing blisters on your fingers and hands after playing the drums, you are likely holding the sticks incorrectly, or too tightly. Review the steps above and try to loosen up your grip and relax.

## BASIC HAND TECHNIQUE

**In this section, we'll learn how to strike the drums.** Go ahead and hold your drumsticks using the matched (German) grip we just learned, and follow these steps.

**1** Place the tip of both sticks right in the center of the snare drum, about an inch above the drumhead. Position your arms so your right stick is between 4 and 5 o'clock on the drum, and your left stick is between 7 and 8 o'clock on the drum. Your palms should be facing the floor, and your forearms should be parallel with the ground and at a 90-degree angle to your upper arms. We'll refer to this as the starting position. Remember to keep your palms facing down.

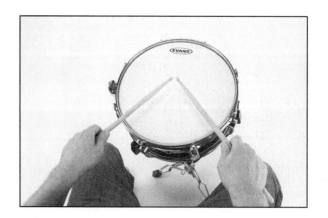

**2** Now, keeping your elbows stationary, raise your right hand and the tip of the drumstick up in the air so it's pointing straight at the ceiling.

**3** Next, keeping your elbows stationary, swing your hand and the drumstick down while simultaneously snapping your wrist towards the floor so the tip of the drumstick strikes the drum right in the center of the head. This motion is similar to what you would do when snapping a whip, or when casting a fishing line.

**4** As soon as the tip of the drumstick hits the center of the drumhead, snap your wrist back up and allow the drumstick to rebound freely off the head so that the tip ends up pointing back up towards the ceiling. It's important to let the stick rebound naturally. You will control and guide the stick after it rebounds off the head, but don't force it up towards the ceiling. You will feel the stick vibrate a bit in your hands when done properly.

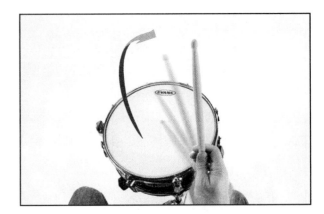

❺ Finally, return your stick to the starting position and repeat the above steps with your left hand using the same technique.

Remember to keep your palms facing down.

If the stick doesn't bounce freely off the head, you may be holding the stick too far forward or too far back in your hand. Try adjusting the stick so a little less front end is showing and see if that fixes it. If that adjustment made it worse, go the other way and adjust the stick so more front end is showing. Experiment with the stick position until you find a nice fulcrum point where the stick bounces freely off the head.

Don't restrict the natural rebound of the stick by digging it into the drumhead. This makes the drum sound awful, and playing with this bad technique can cause injuries in your elbows and wrists. Instead, let the stick bounce freely, and grip the drumsticks just tight enough to keep them from flying out of your hands.

## In this section, we'll learn how to play the kick drum and the hi-hat with your feet.

There are two basic foot techniques for drummers: heel up and heel down.

**Heel up:** This is a technique where the ball of the foot and the toes remain on the pedal at all times, but the heel is raised off the pedal. This is a common technique for drummers who need a lot of volume and power from their kick drum.

**Heel down:** This is a technique in which the bottom of the entire foot is in contact with the pedal at all times. This is a technique commonly used by drummers looking for very soft volume from their kick drum.

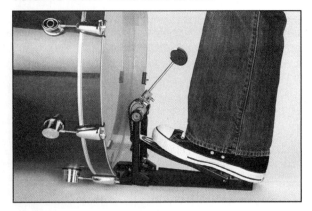 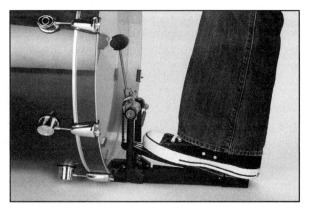

Many drummers switch back and forth freely between these two techniques. You can use either the heel up or heel down technique with your hi-hat foot as well. One technique is not better or worse than the other. It's just a matter of personal preference, so use whichever technique is most comfortable for you.

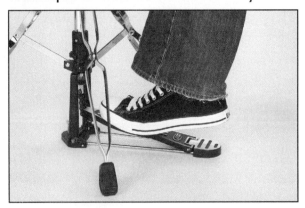 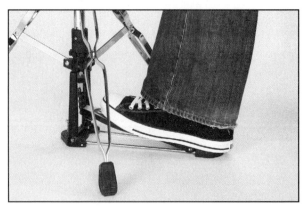

Whether you're playing heel up or heel down, make sure you don't lean your body to the side in any direction. Your upper body should be centered and balanced right over your seat.

**Some drummers read music and some don't.** You don't need to read music in order to play the drums, but it can really accelerate your learning and help you become a great drummer. Learning to read music is similar to learning a language. In music notation, symbols called *notes*, *rests*, and *dynamics* indicate sounds, silence, and punctuation, respectively. These music notation elements can be arranged in all sorts of ways, much like letters of the alphabet are arranged to make words, and how words are arranged to make sentences. Here's how it works.

## Notes

whole note    half note    quarter note    eighth note    sixteenth note

Each type of note represents a different length of time a sound is to be made. A *whole note* is a long sound. A *half note* is a sound that lasts half the time of a whole note. A *quarter note* lasts half as long as a half note. An *eighth note* lasts half the time of a quarter note, and a *sixteenth note* lasts—you guessed it—half the length of an eighth note. Here's how they look another way:

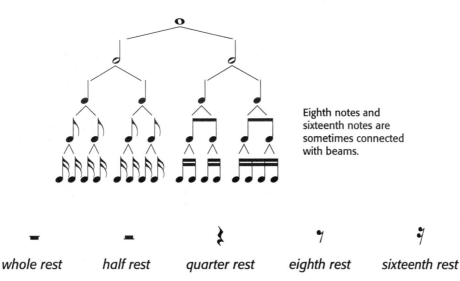

Eighth notes and sixteenth notes are sometimes connected with beams.

## Rests

whole rest    half rest    quarter rest    eighth rest    sixteenth rest

*Rests* work just like notes, except each rest represents a different length of time for silence. Here's how rests are organized:

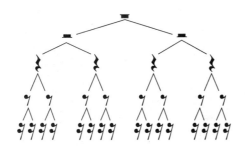

## Beats, Measures, and the Time Signature

A *beat* is a rhythmic term that is used to describe the pulse of the music. When you tap your foot along with music, chances are you are tapping along on the beats.

A *measure* is a specific timeframe of music notation where the beats are expressed with notes and rests. Many measures are arranged together on the page, one after another, to create a song.

A *time signature* is a symbol that describes how beats are organized into measures. A time signature consists of two numbers, one on top of the other, such as $\frac{4}{4}$, $\frac{3}{4}$, and $\frac{12}{8}$.

The number on top tells you how many beats are in a measure. The bottom number tells you which note gets the count; a "1" represents a whole note, a "2" represents a half note, a "4" represents a quarter note, an "8" represents an eighth note, and a "16" represents a sixteenth note.

Most rock songs are written in $\frac{4}{4}$ time: the top number of the time signature is "4," which tells us to count "1–2–3–4" for every measure, and the bottom number is also "4," which tells us the quarter note gets the count. This repeats for each measure, so you count "1–2–3–4|1–2–3–4|1–2–3–4|1–2–3–4" and so on. Each "|" in this example represents the beginning of a new measure.

## The Staff, Bar Lines, Repeat Sign, Clef, and Tempo

A *staff* is the framework upon which notes and rests are written. A staff consists of five lines and looks like this: ≡≡≡

A *bar line* is a vertical line drawn through the staff that divides the staff into measures. There are many bar lines in a piece of music, and each bar line indicates the end of one measure and the beginning of another. A *double bar line* indicates a section break in a piece of music, such as when you go from a verse to a chorus in a song. A *final double bar line* indicates the end of the piece of music.

*bar line        double bar line    final double bar line*

A *repeat sign* has two dots before a final double bar line and indicates that the musician should go back to the opposite-facing repeat sign. If no opposite-facing repeat sign is present, go back to the beginning of the music.

*left-facing repeat    right-facing repeat*

A *clef* is a symbol at the very beginning of a piece of music that tells you the pitch of written notes. The type of clef depends on what instrument the music is written for. The most common clefs are the treble clef 𝄞 and the bass clef 𝄢, but most drum notation uses the neutral clef, which looks like this: ‖

A *tempo marking* indicates the speed at which the music should be played. The tempo generally appears at the beginning of the music and is written like this: ♩ = 90. In this example, the tempo marking is telling us that the quarter note equals 90 beats per minute (*BPM* for short). That is, in one minute of time, there are a total of 90 evenly spaced quarter note beats. A tempo of 200 BPM is very fast, and a tempo of 40 BPM is very slow. A device called a *metronome* is used to determine tempos.

## Putting It all Together

Here's how everything looks when it's all put together. This is the framework for music notation before all the notes and rests are written in.

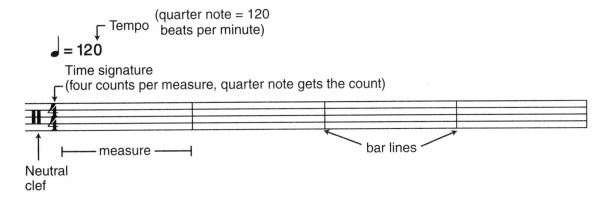

## Writing in the Notes and Rests

Here's how music notation looks when notes and rests are added.

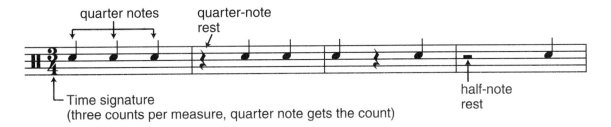

## Drum Notation Key

Now that you know the basic music notation framework and terms used when reading and writing music, let's take a look at how drumset notation is written. Placing a note on a line or space of a staff shows the drummer which part of the drumset to hit. A *drum notation key* is a map that shows which lines and spaces on the staff correspond to the various parts of the drumset.

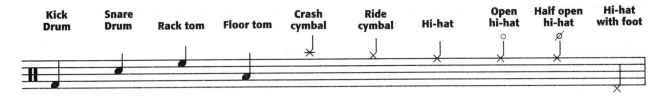

Now you're ready to start playing your first beat. Turn the page, and let's start drumming!

### The Metronome

A *metronome* is a device used to determine tempos. Once you assign a tempo in BPM (beats per minute) into the device, the metronome will emit an audio and/or visual pulse at that tempo. A metronome is a great tool to use when practicing. It will help you develop a good sense of "time" which is one of the most important roles of a drummer. For your convenience, tempo markings have been indicated throughout this book by each example. Try practicing the lessons both with and without a metronome.

# "Dead Leaves and the Dirty Ground"
## FROM THE WHITE STRIPES' *WHITE BLOOD CELLS* (2001)

Meg White lays down a no-nonsense rock drum beat in the opening track of The White Stripes' third studio album, *White Blood Cells*. This song has a time signature of $\frac{4}{4}$, which means that there are four counts per measure, and the quarter note gets the count. Here's how the beat looks when it's written out using music notation.

**Original transcription (0:21):**

Let's start by striking the crash cymbal over and over using the drumstick in your right hand so you're playing quarter notes to the pulse of the music. Your stick should hit the cymbal on what we call the "downbeats," or, in other words, on beats 1, 2, 3, and 4 of each measure.

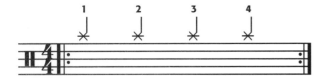

Now, let's continue to strike the crash cymbal on all four beats like the previous example, but this time, let's also strike the snare drum using the stick in your left hand on beats 2 and 4. Pay close attention to making sure both sticks hit their surface at exactly the same time.

Next, let's play the crash cymbal on all four beats, and this time, let's also play the kick drum, but only on beats 1 and 3. Again, pay special attention to making the kick drum and the right hand hit at exactly the same time on beats 1 and 3.

Finally, let's put it all together and play quarter notes on the crash cymbal, the kick drum on beats 1 and 3, and the snare drum on beats 2 and 4. Start slowly at first, and gradually increase the tempo as you feel comfortable until it matches the tempo of the recording.

Congratulations! You just played your very first rock beat!

Along with her band mate Jack, Meg White proved that the two-piece band The White Stripes was mighty enough to top the charts and tour the world. Meg's simple, primal drumming style is the perfect complement to Jack's more "in your face" personality that comes through in his guitar and vocal parts. Meg plays just the right parts at just the right times.

# "Runnin' Down a Dream"
## FROM TOM PETTY'S *FULL MOON FEVER* (1989)

The beat that drummer Phil Jones played in this song is very similar to the beat that was played on "Dead Leaves and the Dirty Ground," but in this tune, the hi-hat is played on the downbeats instead of the crash cymbal, and the tempo is faster. You'll need to swing your left hand under your right so your arms are crossed in order to get your sticks in the right place. Go ahead and give it a try! Start slowly at first, and gradually increase the tempo as you feel comfortable.

**Original transcription (0:01):**

Track 2

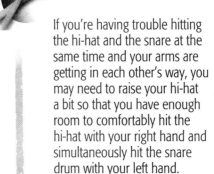

If you're having trouble hitting the hi-hat and the snare at the same time and your arms are getting in each other's way, you may need to raise your hi-hat a bit so that you have enough room to comfortably hit the hi-hat with your right hand and simultaneously hit the snare drum with your left hand.

# "Back in Black"
## FROM AC/DC'S *BACK IN BLACK* (1980)

Phil Rudd started drumming in AC/DC in 1975, and he recorded the drums on some of the band's biggest hits, including this song from their best-selling album. *Back in Black* has sold an estimated 45 million copies to date, making it the second-best-selling album of all time behind Michael Jackson's *Thriller.* Learning to play AC/DC is as important for your rock drumming as water is for your survival. AC/DC drumming is essentially one of the basic food groups of rock drumming, so what are we waiting for? Let's get started!

**Original transcription (0:05):**

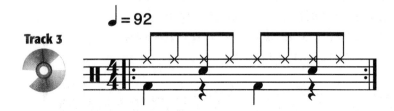

Let's start by playing eighth notes on the hi-hat using your right hand. Start slowly and count along: "1–&–2–&–3–&–4–&." Make sure you hit the hi-hat so the notes are evenly spaced and the volume is consistent from hit to hit.

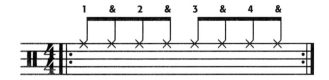

Next, continue playing eighth notes on the hi-hat with your right hand, just like in the previous exercise, but this time, let's also play the snare drum using your left hand on beats 2 and 4.

Now, let's play eighth notes on the hi-hat, and this time, play the kick drum on beats 1 and 3.

Finally, let's put it all together so that you're playing eighth notes on the hi-hat with your right hand, the snare drum on beats 2 and 4 with your left hand, and the kick drum on beats 1 and 3. With a little practice, you'll be playing the rock beat just like Phil Rudd plays it with AC/DC!

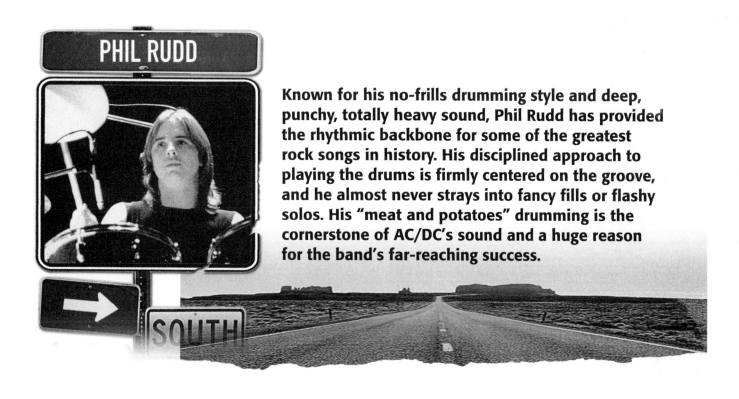

**PHIL RUDD**

Known for his no-frills drumming style and deep, punchy, totally heavy sound, Phil Rudd has provided the rhythmic backbone for some of the greatest rock songs in history. His disciplined approach to playing the drums is firmly centered on the groove, and he almost never strays into fancy fills or flashy solos. His "meat and potatoes" drumming is the cornerstone of AC/DC's sound and a huge reason for the band's far-reaching success.

# "I Won't Back Down"
## FROM TOM PETTY'S *FULL MOON FEVER* (1989)

The beat played in this song is very similar to the beat that was played on "Back in Black," but the tempo is faster in "I Won't Back Down." Start slowly at first, and gradually increase the tempo as you feel comfortable. Notice how drastically different the beat feels simply due to a change in tempo.

**Original transcription (Intro):**

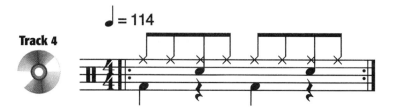

Track 4

♩ = 114

# "Boulevard of Broken Dreams"
## FROM GREEN DAY'S *AMERICAN IDIOT* (2004)

The beat that Tré Cool plays beginning at 0:16 into this song is very similar to the one played on "I Won't Back Down," except on "Boulevard of Broken Dreams," it's played a bit slower and there's an extra kick drum hit added on the "&" of beat 3. Give it a try!

**Original transcription (0:16):**

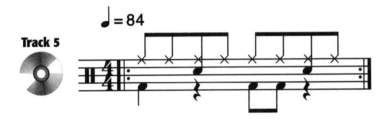

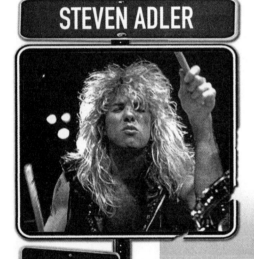

Adler played the drums on Guns N' Roses' 1987 breakthrough multi-platinum album, *Appetite for Destruction*, as well as the band's second multi-platinum release, *Lies*. Adler's power-packed playing style helped propel both albums to the top of the charts, and *Appetite for Destruction* sold over 28 million copies worldwide, making it one of the top-selling albums of all time.

### The Flam

A *flam* is a specific sound where both drumsticks strike the drumhead very close together and in time with one another. If played too close together, the sticks both hit the drumhead at the same time, and that will choke the drum resulting in a dead, dry sound. If the sticks strike the drumhead too far apart, then it sounds like two normal consecutive hits, and not like a flam (it will sound like "bam-bam," instead of "blam"). But when played just right, a flam is an extremely powerful stroke in which both hits can be distinctly heard, but the effect is that the hits are very close together and the drum reacts with a very big, full sound. When notated, a flam looks like this:

# "Paradise City"
## FROM GUNS N' ROSES' *APPETITE FOR DESTRUCTION* (1987)

Any rock music fan that's heard this tune, drummer or not, has a tough time resisting the urge to air drum along with the powerful beat played by Steven Adler at the beginning of "Paradise City." One of the things that make this beat so powerful is the flams that are played on the snare drum.

**Track 6** **Original transcription (0:11):**

Let's start by playing the kick on beats 1 and 3 and on the "&" of beat 3, while playing a flam on the snare on beats 2 and 4. Try to mimic the flam sound as closely as you can, and repeat this exercise until you can play flams comfortably and so they sound like what you hear on the tune.

Now that you have the hang of playing flams, let's play the same beat, but this time remove the kick drum hit on beat 3.

Now, let's put it all together and play the intro beat just like Steven Adler plays it on the recording!

# "You Shook Me All Night Long"
## FROM AC/DC'S *BACK IN BLACK* (1980)

When you compare the written notation, the main beat on this song is similar to the beat that's played on the first two bars of the drum part on "Paradise City." The differences are that in "You Shook Me All Night Long," the tempo is faster, the right hand is playing eighth notes on the hi-hat, and the snare drum is playing on beats 2 and 4 without any flams. Start slowly, and gradually increase the tempo until you can play it comfortably up to speed.

**Original transcription (0:16):**

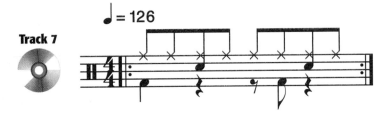

**Track 7**

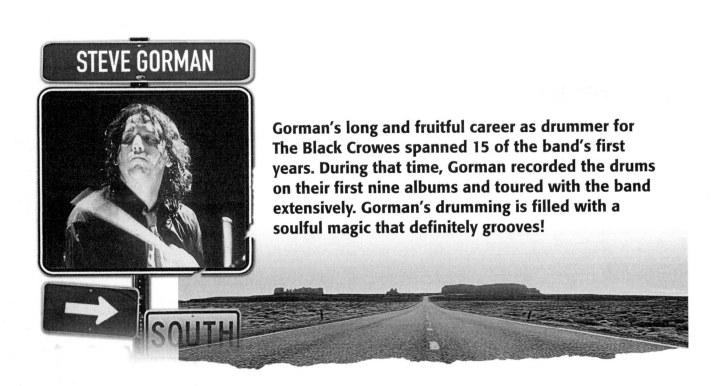

## STEVE GORMAN

Gorman's long and fruitful career as drummer for The Black Crowes spanned 15 of the band's first years. During that time, Gorman recorded the drums on their first nine albums and toured with the band extensively. Gorman's drumming is filled with a soulful magic that definitely grooves!

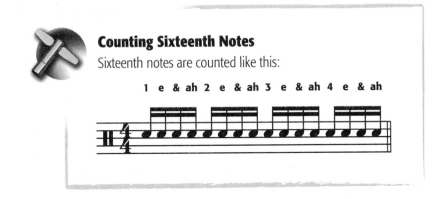

**Counting Sixteenth Notes**

Sixteenth notes are counted like this:

# "Hard to Handle"
## FROM THE BLACK CROWES' *SHAKE YOUR MONEY MAKER* (1990)

This tune was originally recorded and performed by Otis Redding in 1968. The Black Crowes released a harder-edged version in which the drummer, Steve Gorman, played this catchy beat. Note that, when this beat is written out, it looks very similar to AC/DC's "You Shook Me All Night Long," but "Hard to Handle" is played a bit slower and adds a very important snare hit on the "ah" of beat 2. Start slowly, and pay close attention to playing that extra snare hit with the left hand evenly spaced between the hi-hat hits that occur on the "&" of beat 2 and on beat 3.

**Original transcription (Intro):**

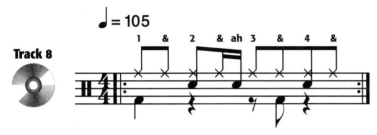

# "Free Fallin'"
## FROM TOM PETTY'S *FULL MOON FEVER* (1989)

Notice how well the kick drum locks in with what the bass guitar is playing in this beat from one of Tom Petty's most popular songs. The two instruments hit together on beat 1 and on the "&" of beat 2, creating a very simple but incredibly strong groove. Give it a try!

**Original transcription (0:35):**

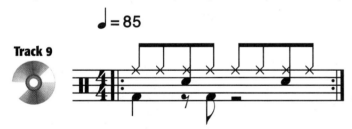

Let's look at this same beat notated a bit differently. Adding the dot to the quarter note means that we can take away the eighth note rest that was included in the previous example. Remember, the actual beat is played exactly the same, whichever way it's written. All we've changed is the way it's notated. Dotted notes are frequently used when notating music because, when you get used to them, they make it easier and quicker to read and play what's written.

**Dotted Notes**

When a dot is added to a note, the duration of that note is extended by half of its value. For example, a quarter note without a dot tells you to play for one full beat. A dotted quarter note tells you to extend that by half its value. Half the value of a quarter note is an eighth note, which can also be thought of as half of one beat. So the dotted quarter note tells us to play for one and a half beats.

# "Come As You Are"
## FROM NIRVANA'S *NEVERMIND* (1991)

Drummer Dave Grohl incorporates a lot of kick drum into the beat of this song from one of the best-selling alternative albums of all time. These kick drum notes help the drums lock in nicely with the guitar and bass parts.

**Original transcription (0:09):**

Let's start by playing eighth notes on the ride cymbal with your right hand, the snare drum on beats 2 and 4 with your left hand, and the kick drum on beats 1 and 3 as well as the "&" of beats 3 and 4.

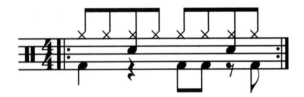

Now, let's change the kick drum pattern so that we play the kick on beat 1 and on the "&" of beats 1, 2, and 3. Slow the beat down if needed, and gradually increase the tempo as you feel comfortable.

Next, let's play the same beat as in the previous exercise, but this time, add another kick hit on the "&" of beat 4.

Finally, put it all together and play the groove just like Dave Grohl plays it on the recording.

**Deep Purple has rotated through numerous lineup changes since forming in 1968, but only one member, drummer Ian Paice, has played with the band every step of the way. Paice was one of the first to bring jazz-inspired technical chops into heavy rock drumming, and he's inspired countless drummers to pick up the sticks and rock.**

# "Smoke on the Water"
## FROM DEEP PURPLE'S *MACHINE HEAD* (1972)

Deep Purple drummer Ian Paice is hailed by many as one of the greatest classic rock drummers of all time. This is the band's most well-known song and houses some amazing drumming by Paice. In fact, this is probably one of the world's most well-known rock songs of all time! This example will introduce you to the two-handed hi-hat rock groove. Let's start by playing alternating strokes on the hi-hat. Start with your right hand and alternate your hands "R–L–R–L."

**Original transcription (0:17):**

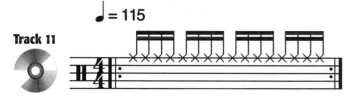

Now, let's continue to the next part of the beat. In this section, Paice adds a snare hit on beats 2 and 4. Play this with the same alternating sticking as in the previous example (R–L–R–L), but move your right stick from the hi-hat to the snare drum on beats 2 and 4. This may be a bit tricky at first, but stick with it until you can play it smoothly and comfortably.

**Original transcription (0:26):**

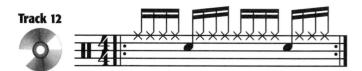

Next, let's add in the kick drum by playing steady eighth notes with your right foot. Notice that you'll be simultaneously hitting the kick drum with every note you play with your right hand.

**Original transcription (0:34):**

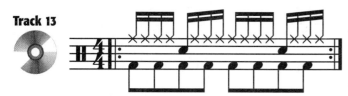

# "Kashmir"
## FROM LED ZEPPELIN'S *PHYSICAL GRAFFITI* (1975)

If one person can hold the title as the greatest, most influential, most emulated rock drummer in history, it has to be Led Zeppelin's late, great drummer, John Bonham. In this tune, Bonham provides a solid and consistent groove that helps give this song the power and mysticism that makes it so special. The groove is played by hitting eighth notes on the hi-hat, the snare on beats 2 and 4, and the kick drum on beats 1 and 3 as well as the "e" of beats 1 and 3. Start slowly, and gradually increase the tempo as you feel comfortable.

**Original transcription (Intro):**

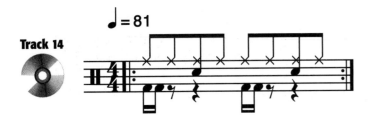

Track 14

♩ = 81

### A "Driving" Beat

"Driving" is a term often used to describe music with intensity or aggression that gives the listener the feeling that the music is being propelled forward.

### A "Laid-Back" Beat

"Laid back" is a term used to describe the opposite effect of a "driving" beat. When a beat is "laid back," it gives the listener the feeling that the music is being pulled back a bit.

Levon Helm was a founding member and hugely creative contributor to The Band, one of the most influential groups of all time. In addition to playing drums with The Band from 1967 to 1976 (and also touring with the legendary Bob Dylan), Helm also sang on some of their biggest hits, including the massively popular song "The Weight."

# "The Weight"
## FROM THE BAND'S *MUSIC FROM BIG PINK* (1968)

Notice that, in the previous groove from the song "Kashmir," the drum beat has a very persistent, driving kind of feel that pushes the song ahead. Bonham achieves that driving feeling in "Kashmir" largely because of the "e" that he plays on the kick drum following the downbeat of beats 1 and 3.

Bonham's driving beat sharply contrasts this beat that Levon Helm plays on The Band's famous 1968 recording "The Weight." The thing that makes the beat in "The Weight" feel drastically different from "Kashmir" is that, in "The Weight," the kick drum is instead played on the "ah" prior to the downbeat of beats 1 and 3. This creates a much more easy-going, laid-back kind of feel.

**Original transcription (0:17):**

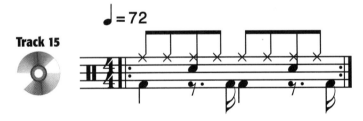

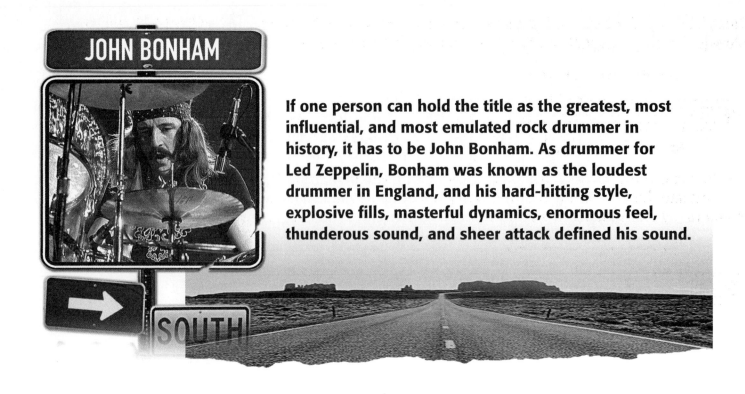

## "When the Levee Breaks"
### FROM LED ZEPPELIN'S *LED ZEPPELIN IV* (1971)

This song beautifully showcases John Bonham's big, powerful sound, and his heavy, feel-good groove. This song was originally recorded in a tall stairwell, which is what gives the drums the echo and very large sound.

**Original transcription (Intro):**

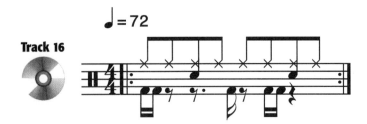

Let's start by playing eighth notes on the hi-hat with your right hand, the snare on beats 2 and 4 with your left hand, and the kick on beat 1, the "e" of beat 1, and on the "&" of beat 3. Start slowly at first, and gradually increase the tempo as you feel comfortable.

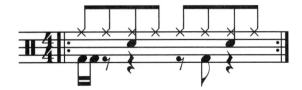

Next, let's take the beat we just played, and add a kick drum hit on the "ah" of beat 3. Again, start slowly, and once you feel comfortable, gradually increase the tempo.

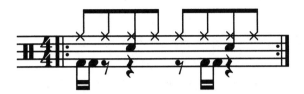

Finally, we'll add one more kick drum hit to the previous beat, this time on the "ah" of beat 2, to complete the groove. Practice this beat, repeating it many times until you can play it very comfortably and so it sounds as close as possible to what Bonham plays on the recording.

### Incorporating the Left Foot

By incorporating your left foot, you can create some fun and interesting sounds with the hi-hat by playing it open, closed, and with only your foot. When notated, an open hi-hat note looks like this:

Sometimes, the hi-hat is played only with your left foot. When notated, a hi-hat played with the foot looks like this:

This notation is also used to indicate when to close the hi-hat after playing it open.

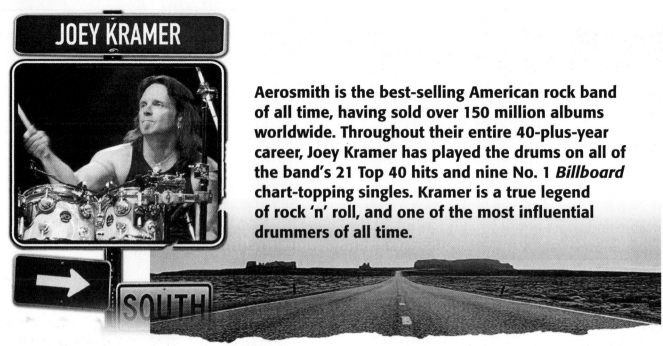

JOEY KRAMER

Aerosmith is the best-selling American rock band of all time, having sold over 150 million albums worldwide. Throughout their entire 40-plus-year career, Joey Kramer has played the drums on all of the band's 21 Top 40 hits and nine No. 1 *Billboard* chart-topping singles. Kramer is a true legend of rock 'n' roll, and one of the most influential drummers of all time.

# "Sweet Emotion"
## FROM AEROSMITH'S *TOYS IN THE ATTIC* (1975)

The beat on this song is provided courtesy of Joey Kramer, legendary rock-solid drummer for Aerosmith since 1970. This is the first beat in which we will incorporate an open hi-hat using your foot.

**Original transcription (0:36):**

Track 17

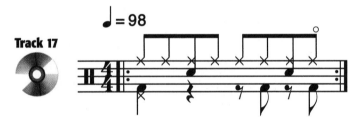

Let's start by playing eighth notes on the hi-hat, the snare on beats 2 and 4, the kick drum on beat 1 and the "&" of beat 3, and an open hi-hat on the "&" of beat 4. To get the open hi-hat in the right place, you'll need to lift your left foot off the hi-hat pedal as you simultaneously hit the hi-hat with your stick on the "&" of beat 4, and then stomp your foot back down on the pedal as you simultaneously hit the hi-hat with your stick on beat 1.

Now, let's play the same beat, but this time, let's add a kick drum hit on the "&" of beat 4. This will be a bit tricky at first since you're stomping your right foot on the kick pedal at the exact same time you're lifting your left foot off the hi-hat pedal. Start slowly and be patient. This may take some time to master, but stick with it and remember— practice makes perfect!

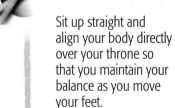

Sit up straight and align your body directly over your throne so that you maintain your balance as you move your feet.

# "Walk This Way"
## FROM AEROSMITH'S *TOYS IN THE ATTIC* (1975)

The beat that kicks off this epic rock classic is another that features a tasty open hi-hat, compliments of Joey Kramer.

**Original transcription (Intro):**

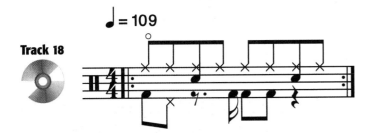

**Track 18**

Let's start by playing eighth notes on the hi-hat with your right hand, the snare on beats 2 and 4 with your left hand, the kick on beats 1 and 3, and an open hi-hat on beat 1. Since the open hi-hat hit is on beat 1, raise your left foot off the hi-hat pedal as you simultaneously hit the hi-hat with your stick on beat 1, and then stomp your foot back down on the hi-hat pedal as you simultaneously hit the hi-hat with your stick on the "&" of beat 1. This will take some practice to perfect, but stick with it. Start slowly, and gradually increase the tempo as you feel comfortable.

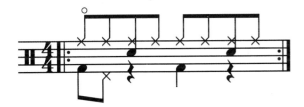

Now that you feel more comfortable playing the basic open hi-hat groove, let's add some spice to the beat by adding a kick drum hit on the "&" of beat 3.

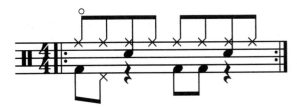

Finally, let's add one last kick drum hit, this time on the "ah" of beat 2, and you'll be playing this legendary beat just like Joey Kramer played it on the recording!

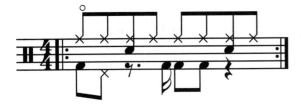

# "Come As You Are"
## FROM NIRVANA'S *NEVERMIND* (1991)

Drummers sometimes make their entrance into a song a little more exciting by playing a short fill before starting the drum groove. In "Come As You Are," Dave Grohl plays this fill before launching into the drum beat that we learned earlier in this book. The fill, like the drum beat, closely follows the guitar part. Give it a try! You'll notice in this transcription that measure two contains only one beat. This is used to illustrate that a crash with a kick drum is to be played on the downbeat of the bar following the fill. Practicing a fill along with the downbeat that follows is a good way to get used to "coming out" of a fill and preparing for the groove that will follow.

**Original transcription (0:07):**

Now, let's play the fill and the drum beat sequentially in context of the song. This example begins with the fill at the entrance of the drum beat, and then goes on to repeat a two-bar drum beat with the fill placed at the end of the second bar.

The release of Nirvana's 1991 album, *Nevermind*, propelled alternative music to the forefront of popular culture, virtually burying the "hair metal" genre that dominated the charts in the preceding decade. The drummer behind it all was Dave Grohl. His explosive energy and highly aggressive, hard-hitting style has inspired thousands of drummers to play.

**PHIL JONES**

Originally hired as their percussionist in 1979, Phil Jones toured with Tom Petty and the Heartbreakers until 1984 and recorded drums on some of the band's biggest hits. Jones's playing feels great on every track he's recorded, and his perfectly chosen beats and fills stand the test of time.

# "Free Fallin'" (ex. 1)
## FROM TOM PETTY'S *FULL MOON FEVER* (1989)

Here's another great example of a drum fill that's used to build some excitement right before the drummer launches into the drum beat. Go ahead and play the fill!

**Original transcription (0:34):**

Now, practice playing the fill in the context of the beat.

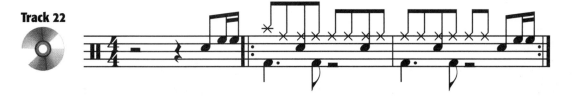

# "Free Fallin'" (ex. 2)

## FROM TOM PETTY'S *FULL MOON FEVER* (1989)

Drum fills are often used to bridge one part of a song to another. For example, Phil Jones plays this drum fill as a bridge between the verse and the first chorus in "Free Fallin'." This transcription repeats a two-bar phrase—the last bar of the verse and the first bar of the chorus—so you can practice playing the drum fill in the context of the beat.

**Original transcription (1:01):**

# "I Won't Back Down"
## FROM TOM PETTY'S *FULL MOON FEVER* (1989)

This tune features a recurring drum fill that's played on the snare, rack tom, kick, and crash cymbal. This same fill is used throughout this song, so once you learn the beat and the fill, you'll be able to play the entire tune!

**Original transcription (0:43):**

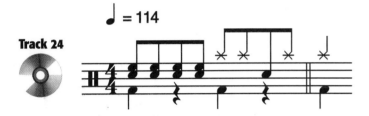

Now, practice playing the fill in the context of the drum beat.

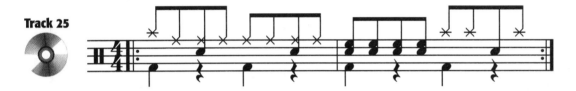

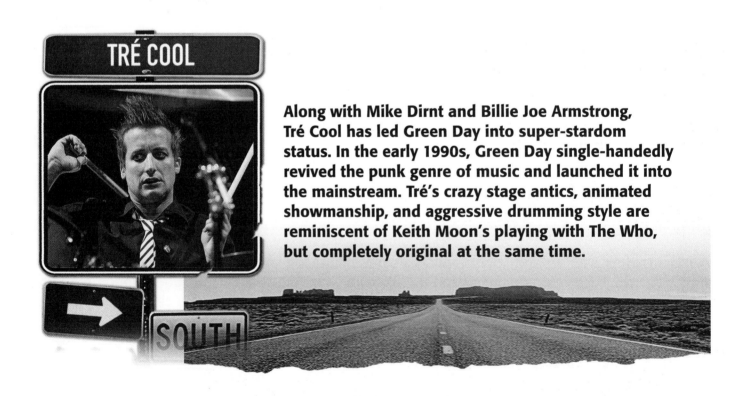

**TRÉ COOL**

Along with Mike Dirnt and Billie Joe Armstrong, Tré Cool has led Green Day into super-stardom status. In the early 1990s, Green Day single-handedly revived the punk genre of music and launched it into the mainstream. Tré's crazy stage antics, animated showmanship, and aggressive drumming style are reminiscent of Keith Moon's playing with The Who, but completely original at the same time.

# "Boulevard of Broken Dreams" (ex. 1)
## FROM GREEN DAY'S *AMERICAN IDIOT* (2004)

Tré Cool plays this catchy fill as he transitions the band into the first two choruses and also into the guitar solo.

**Original transcription (0:48):**

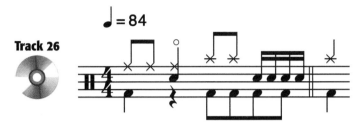

Let's start by playing and repeating the first half of the drum fill for now. Notice that the hi-hat is open on beats 2 and 4, and closed on beats 1 and 3 and on the "&" of beats 1 and 3. You'll need to lift your foot off of the hi-hat pedal on beats 2 and 4 and stomp your foot back down on the pedal on beats 1 and 3 to achieve this.

Next, let's play and repeat the second half of the drum fill.

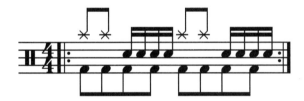

Now, play the entire drum fill, which is one full measure long, and end it with a big simultaneous crash and kick hit on beat 1 of the following measure.

Finally, let's play the drum fill in the context of the drum beat.

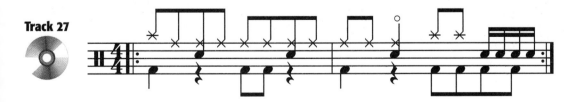

# "Boulevard of Broken Dreams" (ex. 2)
## FROM GREEN DAY'S *AMERICAN IDIOT* (2004)

Here's a cool drum fill Tré plays that incorporates a drag. This drum fill is used to transition the band from the chorus back into the verse.

**Original transcription (1:13):**

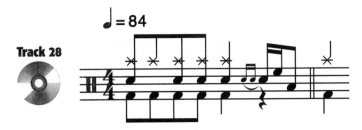

**The Drag**

A *drag* is a sound that's achieved by playing a couple of soft notes on the drum by bouncing one stick immediately followed by a single hit with the other stick. When notated, a drag looks like this:

Let's start by playing the first three beats of the fill and resting on beat 4.

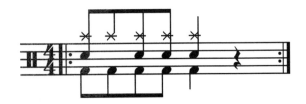

Next, let's practice playing the following example. Pay special attention to the indicated sticking.

Now, let's play the same fill as in the previous example, but this time we'll add a drag leading into beats 2 and 4.

Go ahead and play the entire one-measure drum fill from start to finish and end it by simultaneously hitting the crash and the kick on beat 1 of the following measure.

Finally, let's play the fill within the context of the drum beat.

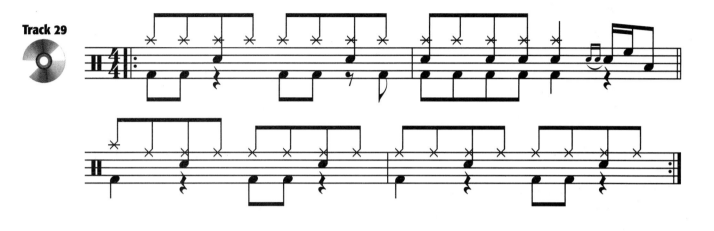

**Track 29**

# "Livin' on the Edge"
## FROM AEROSMITH'S *GET A GRIP* (1993)

Joey Kramer plays a fill in this hit song, from Aerosmith's multi-platinum album *Get a Grip*, that helps the band transition from one section of the tune to the next.

**Original transcription (1:41):**

**Track 30**

Let's begin by playing a version of this fill that strings together a series of sixteenth notes. The first snare hit begins on beat 3 and continues on the snare until moving to the rack tom on the "&" of beat 4. The fill ends with a simultaneous crash and kick hit on beat 1 of the following measure. Go ahead and play through the example.

Now, play the same thing as in the previous lesson, but this time, remove the hit that falls on the "&" of beat 3.

Finally, let's play the fill within the context of the song. Start by playing a beat with quarter notes on the crash cymbal, the snare on beats 2 and 4, and the kick on beats 1 and 3. Then, after the fill, switch from quarter notes on the crash to eighth notes on the hi-hat. This exercise is notated with repeat signs so you can loop this excerpt over and over until you get comfortable using the fill to make the transition from one beat to the next.

**Track 31**

# "Back in Black"
## FROM AC/DC'S *BACK IN BLACK* (1980)

Phil Rudd plays this fill repeatedly on each of the song's verses. The circles with slashes through them above the hi-hat notes indicate that the hi-hats should be played slightly open so that they have a "sloshy" type of sound. Notice how closely it follows the pattern the guitars are playing. Go ahead and give it a try!

**Original transcription (0:14):**

**Track 32**

**ALEX VAN HALEN**

An undisputed legend of rock 'n' roll majesty, Alex Van Halen is a pioneer of the hard rock sound that was born on the Sunset Strip in Los Angeles, California, in the late 1970s. Alex's extreme power, amazing technical ability, unique sound, and incredible showmanship has been praised by millions and has inspired thousands of aspiring drummers to pick up the sticks and play the drums.

# "Jamie's Cryin'"
## FROM VAN HALEN'S *VAN HALEN* (1979)

This tune, from Van Halen's multi-platinum debut album, begins with a drum fill expertly played by the great Alex Van Halen.

**Original transcription (Intro):**

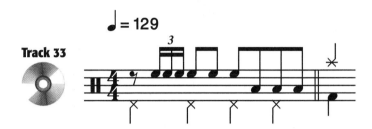

Track 33

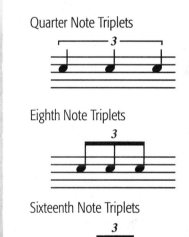

### Triplets

A *triplet* is a group of three notes played in the time of two notes of the same value. Triplets are identified by a small numeral 3 over the note group and are counted just like they sound: tri-pel-let | tri-pel-let | tri-pel-let | tri-pel-let. When notated, triplets look like this:

Quarter Note Triplets

Eighth Note Triplets

Sixteenth Note Triplets

Let's begin by playing a simplified version of the drum fill. Play quarter notes with your foot on the hi-hat to keep time throughout the fill.

Next, let's play it again, but this time, let's add an extra rack tom hit on the "ah" of beat 1.

Now, let's add yet another hit on the rack tom so that a sixteenth note triplet is played starting on the "&" of beat 1. After concluding the fill with a simultaneous crash and kick hit on beat 1, continue by playing the beat from the song as transcribed here.

Track 34

# "D'Yer Mak'er"
## FROM LED ZEPPELIN'S *HOUSES OF THE HOLY* (1973)

John Bonham begins this tune with a drum fill that starts in a rather unusual place—on the "ah" of beat 4.

**Original transcription (Intro):**

Let's get a feel for this drum fill by playing a slightly simplified version, as notated here.

Now, play the fill just like Bonham by adding a snare hit on the "ah" of beat 4, and continue playing the entire next measure of the fill. Also notice that a drag has been added on the "&" of beat 3. Once you can play the fill smoothly and comfortably, try launching right into the drum beat at the end of the fill, as noted here.

# Congratulations! You've just learned to play
# 26 authentic rock beats and fills from some of
# the greatest drummers on the planet!

Now that we've learned the basics of rock drumming and how to play
some very cool beats and fills, let's explore some additional things
about the drums that every drummer should know.

## Acoustic drums all have the same general anatomy as shown below.

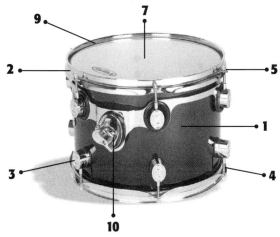
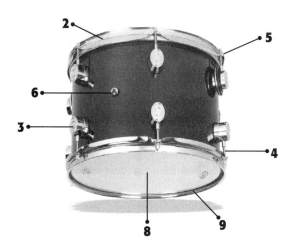

1. Shell
2. Counter hoops
3. Lugs
4. Tension rods
5. Washer
6. Air vent
7. Batter head
8. Resonant head
9. Bearing edge
10. Tom mount

A snare drum is much like any other drum, except it contains additional hardware used to mount snares against the bottom head.

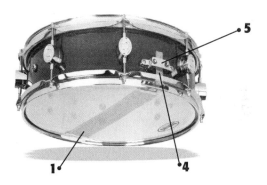

1. Snares
2. Snare strainer / throw-off
3. Snare tension adjuster
4. Tension strap
5. Butt plate

**There are two very basic categories of drumheads:** *batter heads* are the ones on the top of the drums that you strike, and *resonant heads* are the ones on the bottom of the drums that you don't strike.

Within these two broad categories, there are several manufacturers offering a variety of drumhead choices, with each drumhead producing a different sound and a different feel. You don't need to get too wrapped up in this stuff quite yet. Here's a simple rule of thumb: If you hit really hard and play metal or very loud, aggressive music, use a thick double-ply batter head. If you play softer like jazz or moderate rock, then use a thinner single-ply head. The thicker the head, the more durable it will be, but the head will require more force when you hit it in order to get a good tone from it.

Coated Remo Ambassadors or Evans G1 heads on both the batter and resonant sides are popular head selections among many jazz drummers, and clear Remo Emperors or Evans EC2 heads on the batter sides with clear Remo Ambassadors or Evans G1 heads on the resonant sides are popular combinations among many rock and metal drummers. Although many drummers vary their drumhead choices depending on the musical situation at hand, the following chart outlines a basic breakdown of drummers and the general types of heads they use.

| DRUMMER | KICK BATTER | KICK RESONANT | SNARE BATTER | SNARE RESONANT | TOM BATTER | TOM RESONANT |
|---|---|---|---|---|---|---|
| **Tré Cool** (Rock) | DOUBLE PLY | SINGLE PLY | DOUBLE PLY WITH DOT | SINGLE PLY | DOUBLE PLY | SINGLE PLY |
| **Chris Layton** (Blues) | DOUBLE PLY | SINGLE PLY | SINGLE PLY WITH DOT | SINGLE PLY | DOUBLE PLY | SINGLE PLY |
| **Buddy Rich** (Jazz) | SINGLE PLY | SINGLE PLY | SINGLE PLY | SINGLE PLY | SINGLE PLY | SINGLE PLY |

**When a drumhead breaks** or dents and it starts to sound dull and lifeless, it's time to replace it. Generally, you'll replace the resonant heads about a third as often as you'll replace the batter heads. Even though they are not the heads you strike, resonant heads play a huge role in how a drum sounds, so don't overlook the importance of your resonant heads and their role in helping you achieve a great drum sound. The following steps will show you how to replace a drumhead and how to tune a rack tom from scratch. The steps are the same for replacing and tuning a batter head or a resonant head.

**1** Remove the drum from its stand.

**2** Place the drum on a soft, flat surface so the drumhead you're working on is facing up. Resting the drum on a carpeted floor or on a blanket works well. The idea is to make sure that the head you're tuning is the only one you hear when you tap it, and that the head you're not tuning is dampened completely by the surface it's resting on.

**3** Use your drum key to loosen all the lugs and remove the old drumhead.

**4** Wipe down the counter hoops and bearing edges with a soft, dry cloth to remove any dust and debris that may have collected.

**5** Place the new drumhead on the drum.

**6** Put the counter hoop over the drumhead, insert all the lugs, and tighten them with your fingers until they each begin to make contact with the counter hoop. Don't tighten the lugs too much. The idea is to get them into position where the washer on each lug is just barely making contact with the rim of the counter hoop.

**7** Now, use your drum key to tighten the lug closest to you one half turn.

**8** Next, tighten the lug opposite of you one half turn. Continue to tighten each lug sequentially in a star pattern, following the number sequence shown to the right, until each lug has been tightened one half turn.

**9** Lift the drum by the rim and tap the head. If it is loose and doesn't make a clear tone, put the drum back on the soft surface and repeat the half turn, star pattern, lug tightening technique around the drum once again.

**10** Repeat step 9 until you hear a clear tone from the drumhead when you tap it.

**11** Now, place the drum back on the soft surface. Softly and evenly tap the head about an inch and a half from each lug and listen to the resonant pitch.

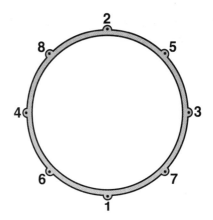

**12** Tighten the lugs near the lower-pitched parts of the drum until they match the higher-pitched parts of the drum. The idea is to fine tune each lug so the resonant pitch is even all around the outer inch and a half of the drum. If one lug is tuned much higher than the others, loosen that lug a quarter turn below where the ending pitch should be, and tighten it slowly until the pitch is where you want it to be.

⓭ Seat the head by applying even pressure on the center of the head with the palm of your hand. You may hear some cracking sounds, and that's ok. You're hearing the sound of the glue cracking around the collar joint on the head and it's completely normal.

⓮ Repeat steps 11 and 12 until the drum is in tune with itself.

⓯ Mount the drum back on its stand and hit it with a drumstick. If you're happy with the sound, you're done tuning! If the sound is too low or too high for your taste, repeat the tuning process to evenly raise or lower the pitch of the head until you find the sound you desire.

Many drummers strive to tune both the batter and resonant heads to the same pitch. You will get different effects if the resonant head is tuned higher or lower in pitch in relation to the batter head. Experiment with different tunings and see what you like.

The same tuning process as outlined above can be used to tune all the drums on your kit, with a couple additional steps on the snare and the kick drums.

After tuning the snare drum, make sure you adjust the snare tension screw so the drum sounds nice and snappy when tapped at a low volume and has a nice crack when struck at a higher volume. If the snare tension is too tight, the drum will sound choked and lifeless. If the snare tension is too loose, the drum will sound distorted and hollow. Experiment with the tension of the snares until you find the sweet spot.

Many drummers also place a small pillow inside the kick drum so it's lightly touching both heads, or they'll place a felt strip between the resonant head and the bearing edges of the kick drum. These muffling techniques help the kick drum produce a nice low, fat, punchy tone. Experiment with different muffling techniques until you find a sound you like.

## DRUMSTICK SELECTION

**There are thousands of different types of drumsticks** sold today in all different sizes, shapes, and materials. Some drummers, like Tommy Lee and Alex Van Halen, use very large drumsticks. Other drummers, like Steve Jordan and Peter Erskine, use very small drumsticks. Most drummers use a stick that falls somewhere in between these extremes. A good basic drumstick to start with is a wood stick made from hickory, size 5A or size 5B. This is a standard material and size and is available from a variety of manufacturers.

As you develop your skills, you may choose to switch between sticks of various sizes or shapes or materials to best suit your particular needs. Most drummers that play hard rock or metal will choose a large stick, like a size 2B. Most drummers that play jazz or very soft rock prefer smaller, lighter sticks, like a size 7A.

**I'd like to thank everyone** who helped bring this book to fruition. I am extremely grateful for each and every contribution, no matter how small, and your help is sincerely appreciated. Without your encouragement and support, this book would never have been possible.

I dedicate this book to my parents, Bob and Mary Jean, who helped me take the first steps down my drumming path. When I showed an interest in playing the drums, you were there to help me. When I needed a teacher, you hooked me up with one of the best around. And when I needed some encouragement, you were there supporting me every step of the way. Thank you for your patience as you listened to me fumble through the first several years of rushed fills, the repetitive beats that I played a zillion times, and my shortcomings when I didn't have even a faint concept of what it meant to groove. You helped empower what became a life-long passion and I thank you from the bottom of my heart for giving me that opportunity.

I also dedicate this book to my sisters, Janet and Chris; and my brothers-in-law, Sam and Scott, who each encouraged me to write my own path regardless of how difficult it may have been at times; and to the love of my life, my wonderful wife Nikki Lackowski, a constant source of love and encouragement, and an amazing woman who never stops believing in me or my talents.

Thanks to my friends and everyone that I've ever had the privilege of making music with, including Nikki O'Neill, Josh "Cartier" Cutsinger, Jon Sfondilis, Matt Hannon, Chris Moseman, Matt Lapperre, Tish Ciravolo, Ron Manus, Tommy Norton, Harold Branch, Jedd Scher, Cale Reese, Mark Ruppe, Paul Stabler, Todd Janko, and so many others who have embarked on various musical journeys with me. And thanks to every drummer mentioned in this book, and countless others who have inspired me to pick up the sticks and play the greatest instrument in the world.

A very special thanks to Ron Manus, a dear friend and a fun mentor; John O'Reilly Jr., Link Harnsberger, Holly Fraser, Mark Burgess, Kate Westin, Ted Engelbart, Glyn Dryhurst, Dave Black, Gwen Bailey-Harbour, Antonio Ferranti, Mike Finkelstein, Daniel Frohnen, Samantha Ordoñez, Ann Miranda, and the entire team at Alfred Music Publishing; Neil Larrivee and Mark Wessels at Vic Firth; Steve Lobmeier, Trish Johnson, Jim Bailey, Michael Robinson and all the wonderful people at Evans Drumheads; Don Lombardi, Juels Thomas, and Scott Donnell at DW Drums; John DeChristopher and Sarah Malaney at Zildjian; Frank Corniola and all the wonderful people at *Drumscene*; all the great folks at *Modern Drummer*; Phil Hood, Andy Doerschuk, and the folks at *DRUM!*; everyone at *Drumhead, Drummer, Rhythm*, and *Percussioni* magazines; Bernhard Castiglioni at Drummerworld.com; Mike Dolbear at MikeDolbear.com; Tiger Bill Meligari at TigerBill.com; Bart Elliott at DrummerCafe.com; Martin Osborne at Onlinedrummer.com; John Coia at Drum.com; Bob Gatzen; all the readers of *Modern Drummer* magazine and the readers of *DRUM!* magazine who voted for *On the Beaten Path: The Drummer's Guide to Musical Styles and the Legends Who Defined Them* as the "No. 1 Educational Book" in both of their 2008 Reader's Polls and who voted for *On the Beaten Path: Progressive Rock* among the winners in both of their 2009 Reader's Polls; and to Dean Turner, my first drum teacher who led me on my first steps down the beaten path. I thank you all from the bottom of my heart.

—Rich Lackowski

# Congratulations!

You have completed **Level 1** of the *On the Beaten Path: Beginning Drumset Course.* **Level 2** explores **dozens** of authentic blues and jazz beats and fills played by **drumming legends** including

**Art Blakey** (Art Blakey & The Jazz Messengers, Thelonious Monk), **"Philly" Joe Jones** (Miles Davis), **Steve Jordan** (The Blues Brothers), **Chris Layton** (Stevie Ray Vaughan and Double Trouble), **Mitch Mitchell** (The Jimi Hendrix Experience), **Buddy Rich** (Buddy Rich Big Band), and **Max Roach** (Miles Davis, Clifford Brown). **Plus,** you'll learn about double-stroke (open) rolls, multiple bounce (closed/buzz/press) rolls, the 9-stroke roll, accents, rim clicks, ghost notes, crescendos, and decrescendos.

And you'll learn valuable concepts like call and response, reading and playing cues, and improvisation. So, what are you waiting for? Let's get started on **Level 2!**

*Audio examples performed by Rich Lackowski.*
*Instructional photos by Larry Lytle.*

# "Red House"
## FROM THE JIMI HENDRIX EXPERIENCE'S *ARE YOU EXPERIENCED* (1997 REMASTERED VERSION)

Much of early rock 'n' roll was rooted in the blues, and this classic song by Jimi Hendrix is a great example of a blues tune with a good, solid blues drum beat, beautifully played by the late great Mitch Mitchell. The tune is from the album *Are You Experienced*, which VH1 named the 5th greatest album of all time and *Rolling Stone* magazine ranked no. 15 on their "500 Greatest Albums of All Time" list. This song was originally omitted on the USA version of the 1967 release, but fortunately made its way onto the 1997 U.S. remastered edition.

**Original transcription (0:16):**

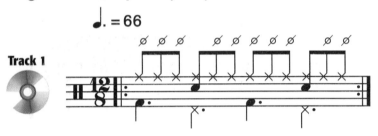

Track 1

This tune is in $\frac{12}{8}$ which means there are 12 beats per measure and the eighth note gets the count. Let's start by playing eighth notes on the hi-hat with your right hand to the pulse of the music. Start by counting along with each hit:

**1**–2–3–**4**–5–6–**7**–8–9–**10**–11–12 | **1**–2–3–**4**–5–6–**7**–8–9–**10**–11–12

and so on. The circles with the slashes through them that are above the hi-hat notes indicate that the hi-hats should be played slightly open so that they have a "sloshy" type of sound. Let's give it a try!

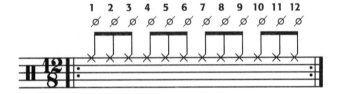

Next, let's add a kick drum hit on beats 1 and 7. Start slowly, and gradually increase the tempo as you feel comfortable.

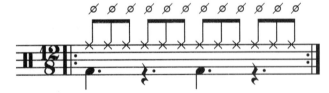

Now, let's add a snare drum hit with your left hand on beats 4 and 10.

Finally, close the hi-hat on beats 4 and 7 by stepping on the hi-hat pedal with your foot, and you'll be playing the blues just like Mitch Mitchell does on the recording.

Congratulations! You just learned to play your first blues beat!

MITCH MITCHELL

Mitchell mastered the delicate balance of keeping the groove fluid, yet solid, while simultaneously packing in his share of solos and fills around Jimi Hendrix's guitar. The result was an extremely complementary chemistry in musicianship, where the dynamics and emotional impact of the songs were greatly intensified. Mitchell played the drums on every Jimi Hendrix Experience recording and he was Jimi's longest-running and most important creative partner.

# "You Shook Me"
## FROM LED ZEPPELIN'S *LED ZEPPELIN* (1969)

John Bonham lays down a nice heavy blues beat in this legendary tune from Led Zeppelin's debut album. Notice that this groove, like the previous one, is in $\frac{12}{8}$. This is a very standard time signature for many blues songs and something you'll see a lot more of as you continue to play the blues.

**Original transcription (0:05):**

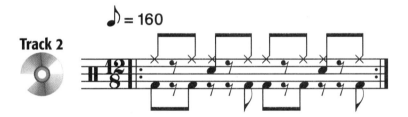

Let's start by playing the beat we just learned in "Red House," but this time, let's play it a little slower, and with the hi-hats fully closed.

Next, let's remove some of the hits on the hi-hat. For this example, just play the hi-hat on beats 1, 3, 4, 6, 7, 9, 10, and 12. Listen to the way Bonham plays it on the recording and mimic along.

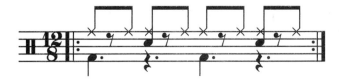

Now, add kick drum hits on beats 3 and 9.

Finally, add some more kick drum hits, this time on beats 6 and 12, and you'll be playing the deep powerful blues groove just like John Bonham plays with Led Zeppelin!

# "Paying the Cost to Be the Boss"
## FROM B.B. KING'S *COMPLETE COLLECTION* (2008, SINGLE VERSION ORIGINALLY RELEASED IN 1968)

This tune by B.B. King, one of the greatest bluesmen of all time, features the shuffle beat. This is an important beat that you'll encounter many times as you continue to play the drums, and it's the cornerstone of many blues and early rock tunes. Listen closely to how drummer Sonny Freeman plays this beat, and then give it a try yourself!

**Original transcription (Intro):**

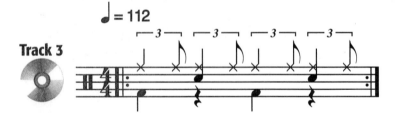

Notice that this beat is a bit similar to "You Shook Me," except it's played faster and, in this example, there are a few less kick drum hits. In general, it is easier and more common for slower blues grooves like "Red House" and "You Shook Me" to be written and played in $\frac{12}{8}$ and for faster blues/shuffle grooves like "Paying the Cost to Be the Boss" to be written and played in $\frac{4}{4}$. There are several ways you'll see this shuffle beat written, so, to prepare you for these situations, the most common notations are listed here. Remember that, even though the way the beat is notated varies, the actual shuffle beat is played the same in all cases.

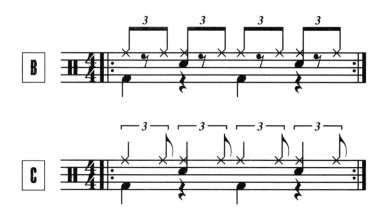

Throughout this book, we'll notate these types of shuffle grooves like you see it in the example below, which is based on triplets. Now go ahead and play the shuffle beat. Start slowly, and gradually increase the tempo until you can play along with the recording.

# "Sweet Home Chicago"
## FROM THE BLUES BROTHERS' *THE BLUES BROTHERS SOUNDTRACK* (1980)

This blues standard features another shuffle beat, sometimes called a shuffle with "four on the floor," which refers to the kick drum being played on all four beats. This shuffle beat, masterfully performed by drummer Steve Jordan, is similar to "Paying the Cost to Be the Boss," but "Sweet Home Chicago" is played a bit faster and a bit more driving with "four on the floor." Give it a try! Like the previous beats, it's best to master the groove slowly and then gradually increase the tempo until you can play along with the original recording.

**Original transcription (0:07):**

Track 4

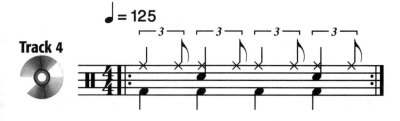

# "Revolution"
## FROM THE BEATLES' *1967-1970 (THE BLUE ALBUM)* (1973, ORIGINALLY RELEASED IN 1968 AS THE B-SIDE TO THE "HEY JUDE" SINGLE)

So far, our hands have been busy playing the bouncy shuffle beats on the hi-hat. Let's give our hands a rest and try playing the bouncy shuffle beat with our foot instead. Although this song is not often attributed to being in the blues genre, the drum beat masterfully performed by Ringo Starr has a definite blues shuffle quality to it, and it's a great groove to get that kick drum foot in shape!

Start by playing this very slowly, and gradually increase the tempo as you feel comfortable. If any of your muscles start to cramp up, reduce the tempo and try to relax as you play the groove. Try to make your limbs flow in a relaxed motion instead of forcing everything.

**Original transcription (0:08):**

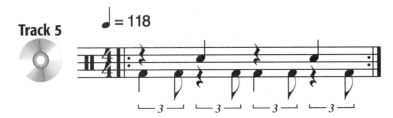

Track 5

Remember to keep breathing! Some people have the bad habit of holding their breath when they play more difficult passages. This just deprives your muscles of oxygen, which is vital to keep them from cramping up. Breathe!

RINGO STARR

In addition to being the drummer in The Beatles, the greatest and most influential band of all-time, Ringo was also a great innovator. He was the leading pioneer that broke rock music out of the jazz/swing-rooted styles commonly found in the music of Chuck Berry, Elvis Presley, and Little Richard, and he was one of the first drummers to popularize performing on a drum riser, playing with matched grip, and tuning his drums low and using muffling techniques.

# "Bad to the Bone"
## FROM GEORGE THOROGOOD & THE DESTROYERS' *BAD TO THE BONE* (1982)

This tune features a drum beat, played on the recording by Jeff Simon, that's very similar to what we just played on "Revolution," but "Bad to the Bone" is a bit slower and adds triplets on the hi-hats. Start slowly, and increase the speed only after you've mastered the drum beat at a slower tempo.

**Original transcription (0:08):**

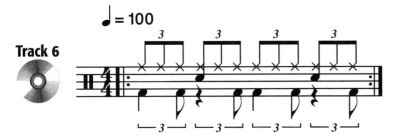

### Accented Notes

An *accented note* is played louder than the other notes around it. When notated, an accented note looks like this:

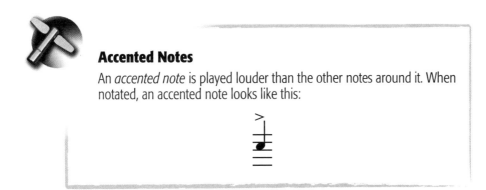

# "Who Do You Love"
## FROM GEORGE THOROGOOD & THE DESTROYERS' *MOVE IT ON OVER* (1978)

Although slow $\frac{12}{8}$ beats and quicker shuffle beats are commonly featured in blues tunes, there are plenty of other ways for drummers to play the blues. This tune features an accented floor tom groove that creates a drum beat quite different than any of the beats we've learned so far.

**Original transcription (0:04):**

Start by playing quarter notes with your foot on the hi-hat.

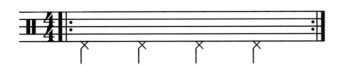

Next, play the following pattern on the floor tom while playing quarter notes on the hi-hat with your foot. Pay attention to the indicated sticking. These hits on the floor tom lock in tightly with the tune, so listen and play along.

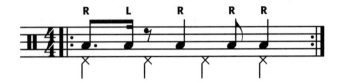

Now, add the following floor tom hits, again paying special attention to the indicated sticking.

Next, let's add a few more floor tom hits, again paying special attention to the indicated sticking.

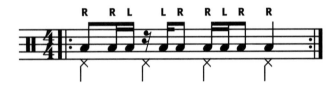

Let's play it again with all of the floor tom hits.

Finally, play it with accents on the indicated beats. These accents lock in tightly with the tune, so listen and play along. Practice this beat until you can play it smoothly and comfortably.

# "Boom, Boom"
## FROM JOHN LEE HOOKER'S *URBAN BLUES* (1967)

This classic tune by one of the greatest blues legends of all time features another beat that doesn't fall into the traditional categories of slow $\frac{12}{8}$ grooves or the faster shuffle beats that make up so much of blues music. Drummer Al Duncan crafted this drum beat, which perfectly fits the rhythm and attitude of the song.

**Original transcription (Intro):**

Let's begin by playing the hi-hat and the kick drum on beats 2, 3, and 4 of the first measure, and on beat 1 of the second measure.

Next, let's add snare hits on beats 3 and 4 of the first measure, and on beat 1 of the second measure.

Finally, add a snare hit on the "let" of the triplet that starts on beat 1, and you'll be playing the drum beat just like it was played on this classic blues track.

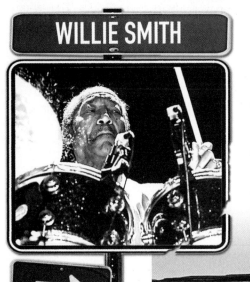

Drummer for Muddy Waters for nearly two decades, Willie Smith appears on all of Waters's Grammy award-winning albums, including *Hard Again, I'm Ready, They Call Me Muddy Waters, Muddy "Mississippi" Waters Live, The London Muddy Waters Sessions,* and *The Muddy Waters Woodstock Album.* Smith is one of the pillars of blues drumming, and a true legend of the instrument.

# "I Want to Be Loved #2"
## FROM MUDDY WATERS' *HARD AGAIN* (1977)

Drummer Willie Smith integrates a short triplet drum fill right into the drum beat of this song, which was written by the mighty bluesman Willie Dixon, and performed here by "the father of Chicago blues," Muddy Waters.

**Original transcription (Intro):**

Let's start by getting comfortable playing the basic blues beat before adding the triplet snare fills.

Now, let's add that triplet fill that comes at the end of the two-bar phrase, beginning on the "let" of beat 3 in bar 2.

Finally, set up the song by playing a triplet on the snare starting on beat 4, before launching into beat 1 of the repeating two-bar drum groove.

# "Manish Boy"
## FROM MUDDY WATERS' *HARD AGAIN* (1977)

The true essence of the blues is wonderfully captured on this recording by Muddy Waters. Muddy begins the tune with a *call and response* between his voice and his guitar. Call and response describes a sequence of two musical phrases where the second phrase is an artistic imitation or reflection of the first musical phrase. Waters makes the call with his voice—"oh yeah"—and the response with his guitar while other musicians and spectators holler out their enthusiastic praise before Muddy unleashes his excited and authoritative "Wooooooo!" that cues the rest of the band to join in and play along.

**Original transcription (0:29):**

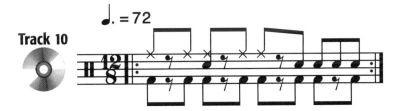

**Track 10**

Let's start by playing a slow $\frac{12}{8}$ blues beat, where the kick drum is played simultaneously with the hi-hats, and the snare is played on beats 4 and 10.

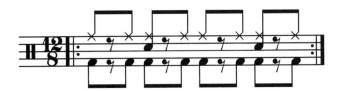

Next, let's play the same beat, but this time, play beats 9, 10, and 12 on the snare drum instead of on the hi-hat.

Finally, play the same beat as in the previous lesson but this time, add a snare hit on beat 11, and you'll be playing the blues groove just like Willie Smith plays it on the recording!

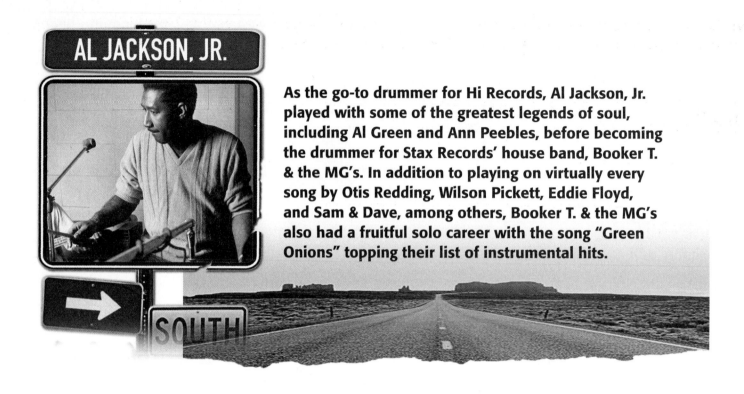

As the go-to drummer for Hi Records, Al Jackson, Jr. played with some of the greatest legends of soul, including Al Green and Ann Peebles, before becoming the drummer for Stax Records' house band, Booker T. & the MG's. In addition to playing on virtually every song by Otis Redding, Wilson Pickett, Eddie Floyd, and Sam & Dave, among others, Booker T. & the MG's also had a fruitful solo career with the song "Green Onions" topping their list of instrumental hits.

# "Green Onions"
## FROM BOOKER T. & THE MG'S *GREEN ONIONS* (1962)

Al Jackson Jr. was the drummer in the band Booker T. & the MG's, the house band for Stax records, who provided the music foundation for many of the best blues, soul, and R&B acts to come out of Memphis. "Green Onions" is one of the band's most popular hits and is a great tune that demonstrates how a relatively simple-looking beat can actually be quite difficult to master.

**Original transcription (0:07):**

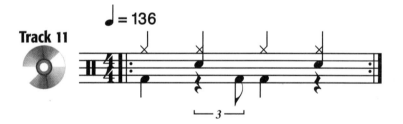

Let's begin by playing quarter notes on the ride cymbal, the kick on beats 1 and 3, and the snare on beats 2 and 4.

Now, add a kick hit on the "let" of beat 2. You may have to practice this slowly at first before increasing the tempo, but, with a little patience, you'll be playing the groove just like Al Jackson Jr.!

### Wire Brushes

*Wire brushes* are special "sticks" used by drummers to achieve a softer sound. Wire brushes have a wood, plastic, or rubber handle with dozens of thin wires fanning out on the opposite end. Unlike drumsticks, which are made of wood and therefore achieve a loud, defined sound when they strike a cymbal or drumhead, wire brushes achieve a soft, warm sound.

# "At Last" (ex. 1)
## FROM ETTA JAMES'S *AT LAST* (1961)

Etta James delivers one of the world's greatest blues performances on this track from her debut album. The drummer plays between two basic grooves. In this transcription, we'll focus on the first and simpler of the two grooves. The softer drum sound you hear on the recording is achieved by playing with wire brushes instead of drumsticks.

**Original transcription (0:21):**

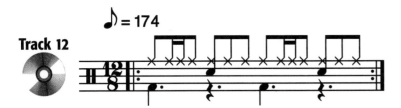

Let's begin by playing a basic $\frac{12}{8}$ groove.

Now, add an extra hi-hat hit evenly spaced between beats 2 and 3 and between beats 8 and 9. You can count this as "1–2–&–3–4–5–6–7–8–&–9–10–11–12." Give it a try!

# "At Last" (ex. 2)
## FROM ETTA JAMES'S *AT LAST* (1961)

Some sections of this tune demand a bit more intensity in the drum beat. Notice how the drum groove gets a little busier at 0:55.

**Original transcription (0:55):**

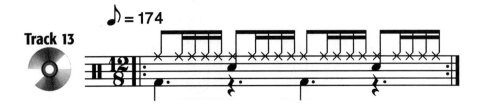

Let's start by playing the first drum groove we learned on the previous transcription.

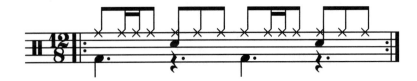

Now, let's add an extra hi-hat hit evenly spaced between beats 3 and 4, and another hi-hat hit between beats 9 and 10.

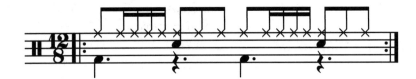

Finally, apply that busy, bouncy hi-hat to these other sections of the groove, and with a little practice, you'll have learned everything you need to know to play along with this classic blues tune.

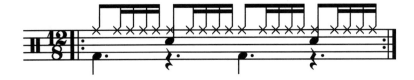

# "Texas Flood"
## FROM STEVIE RAY VAUGHAN AND DOUBLE TROUBLE'S *TEXAS FLOOD* (1983)

Chris Layton had the divine privilege of playing the drums for one of the greatest blues guitarists of all time—Stevie Ray Vaughan. Layton is a gifted blues drummer with a talent for laying down the perfect drum groove to complement Stevie's brilliant playing. Check out the groove Layton plays in this popular tune from Vaughan's debut album.

**Original transcription (0:01):**

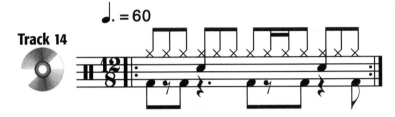

Let's start by playing a simplified $\frac{12}{8}$ blues groove with steady eighth notes on the ride cymbal, snare on beats 4 and 10, and kick on beats 1, 3, 7, and 9.

Next, let's add an additional hit on the ride cymbal that's spaced between beats 8 and 9. To play beat 9 and the hit that precedes it quickly enough, you'll need to bounce the stick off the cymbal. Start by hitting the ride cymbal like you normally would with the whipping, or casting, motion, but this time, let the stick bounce off the surface. The next step is to try it again, but this time, after the stick hits the cymbal and bounces once, tighten your fingers and catch the drumstick as you lift it off the surface. This "snap, bounce, catch" motion will help you play faster patterns like this, and will also help you learn to play drum rolls later. Let's try playing this beat with the "snap, bounce, catch" technique. Practice slowly at first and be patient. You can do this!

Finally, add one more kick hit on beat 12, and you'll be playing the same drum beat that Chris Layton plays on the song!

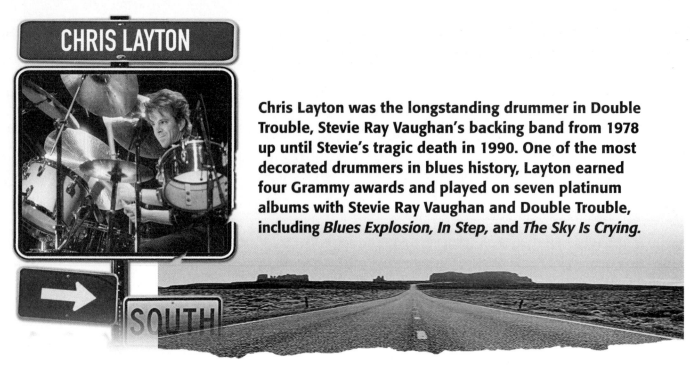

**Chris Layton** was the longstanding drummer in Double Trouble, Stevie Ray Vaughan's backing band from 1978 up until Stevie's tragic death in 1990. One of the most decorated drummers in blues history, Layton earned four Grammy awards and played on seven platinum albums with Stevie Ray Vaughan and Double Trouble, including *Blues Explosion, In Step,* and *The Sky Is Crying.*

# "Pride and Joy"
## FROM STEVIE RAY VAUGHAN AND DOUBLE TROUBLE'S *TEXAS FLOOD* (1983)

Chris Layton plays a commanding shuffle beat that's loaded with some very tasty snare drum work. Notice all the soft ghost note hits on the snare drum that fall between the loud accented backbeats on 2 and 4.

**Original transcription (0:07):**

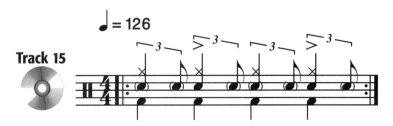

Track 15

First, let's break the beat down into its most basic elements by playing quarter notes on the ride and the kick, and the snare on beats 2 and 4.

**Ghost Notes**

A *ghost note* is played softer than the other notes around it.

When notated, a ghost note looks like this:

Next, let's add ghost notes on the snare drum on beats 1 and 3. Try to create a very big difference in volume between the ghost notes on beats 1 and 3 and the accented notes on beats 2 and 4.

Now, let's add some more ghost notes on the snare, this time on the "let" of beats 2 and 4. Practice this at a very slow tempo, and gradually increase the speed as you feel comfortable.

Finally, let's add additional snare ghost notes on the "let" of beats 1 and 3. This is a bit tricky at first and requires you to play a very soft note quickly followed by a very loud note, all with your left hand. Start by playing this groove at a very slow tempo and pay close attention to playing the ghost notes very soft and the accented notes very loud. These dynamics, or contrasts in volume, is what make the beat really groove, so practice this until you can play it comfortably. Playing this beat will also develop strength and dexterity in your left hand, which will help you become a better drummer. So stick with it and you will see positive results!

# "Move It On Over"
## FROM GEORGE THOROGOOD & THE DESTROYERS' *MOVE IT ON OVER* (1978)

You may notice that the drum groove in this tune is very similar to the beat Bonham plays on Led Zeppelin's "You Shook Me," except for one major thing—"Move It On Over" is faster—much, MUCH faster!

**Original transcription (0:07):**

Track 16

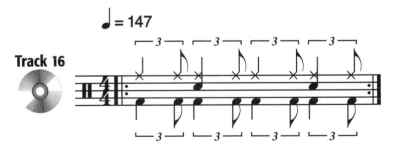

Let's build up our endurance by first focusing on the hi-hat. Start by playing this beat at a comfortable tempo, and gradually increase the speed until you reach the tempo of the song. Practice playing the beat at the marked tempo until you can play it for 60 seconds straight, and remember to relax if you feel your arm starting to tense up.

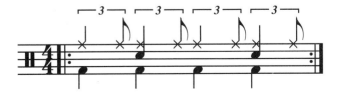

Now, let's work on building your endurance by focusing on the kick drum. Again, start by playing this beat at a comfortable tempo and gradually increase the speed until you reach the tempo of the song. Practice playing the beat at the marked tempo until you can play it for 60 seconds straight, and remember to relax if you feel your foot starting to tense up.

Now that we've built up your endurance separately on both the hi-hat and the kick drum, it's time to put both parts together. You may have to start at a slower tempo, but with some practice, you'll be playing this smokin' shuffle beat just like Jeff Simon plays it on the recording!

## BASIC BLUES AND SHUFFLE FILLS

# "You Shook Me"
## FROM LED ZEPPELIN'S *LED ZEPPELIN* (1969)

John Bonham plays a simple eighth-note fill on the snare, floor tom, and kick to set up the beat he plays for the remainder of the tune. Let's begin by playing the drum fill and ending it with a simultaneous kick and crash hit on beat 1 of the following measure.

**Original transcription (0:04):**

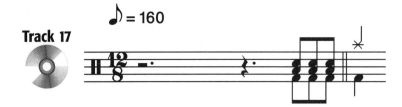

Now, play the beat after you play the fill, just like Bonham played it on the recording.

# "Bad to the Bone"
## FROM GEORGE THOROGOOD & THE DESTROYERS' *BAD TO THE BONE* (1982)

Jeff Simon's fill on the intro of "Bad to the Bone" builds on the same type of fill that Bonham played on "You Shook Me" and adds some embellishments that closely tie in with George Thorogood's catchy guitar riff. Let's try playing the fill by itself, ending with a simultaneous kick and crash hit on beat 1 of the following measure.

**Original transcription (0:06):**

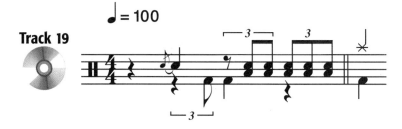

Now, try playing the fill right into the beat of the song, just like it's played on the original recording.

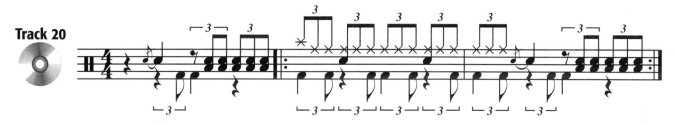

# "Texas Flood"
## FROM STEVIE RAY VAUGHAN AND DOUBLE TROUBLE'S *TEXAS FLOOD* (1983)

Chris Layton cues the band with this short fill that starts with a drag on the snare on beat 10, carries through with high tom and floor tom hits on beats 11 and 12, respectively, and ends with a simultaneous kick and ride hit on beat 1 of the following measure. Go ahead and try playing the drum fill just like Layton plays it on the recording.

**Original transcription (Intro):**

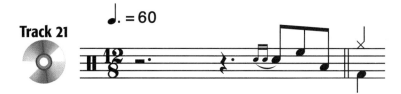

Now, try playing the drum fill as smoothly as you can, right into the drum beat for the song. Notice that a very similar drum fill occurs at the end of measure 2 of the tune. Practice the fill that leads into the beat, and also the fill leading out of the beat, until you can play them both comfortably and smoothly.

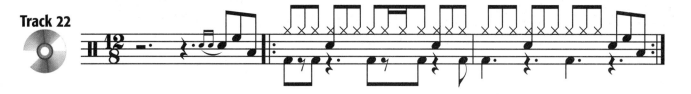

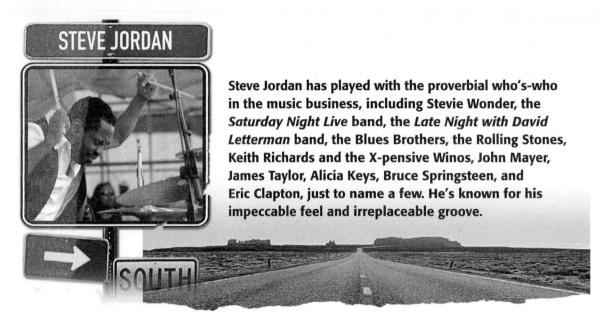

Steve Jordan has played with the proverbial who's-who in the music business, including Stevie Wonder, the *Saturday Night Live* band, the *Late Night with David Letterman* band, the Blues Brothers, the Rolling Stones, Keith Richards and the X-pensive Winos, John Mayer, James Taylor, Alicia Keys, Bruce Springsteen, and Eric Clapton, just to name a few. He's known for his impeccable feel and irreplaceable groove.

# "Sweet Home Chicago" (ex. 1)
## FROM THE BLUES BROTHERS' *THE BLUES BROTHERS SOUNDTRACK* (1980)

This song is built on a standard 12-bar blues form, which means the band plays sections that are in groups of 12 bars (measures). At the end of the 12th bar, there is something called a *turnaround*. The turnaround is a special fill that concludes the first 12-bar section and sets up the next 12-bar section. This is a very common musical element you will encounter as you listen to the blues. In this example, Steve Jordan plays the following turnaround fill, as notated here. Go ahead and try to play this fill on your own.

**Original transcription (0:29):**

Now, here's how the entire 12-bar section looks when it's notated on paper. Notice that the same fill we just learned is now placed in measure 12 of this 12-bar blues section. Go ahead and play, then repeat, the entire section. It may be helpful to either play along with the song on your headphones or sing to yourself while you play along on the drums.

**Track 24**

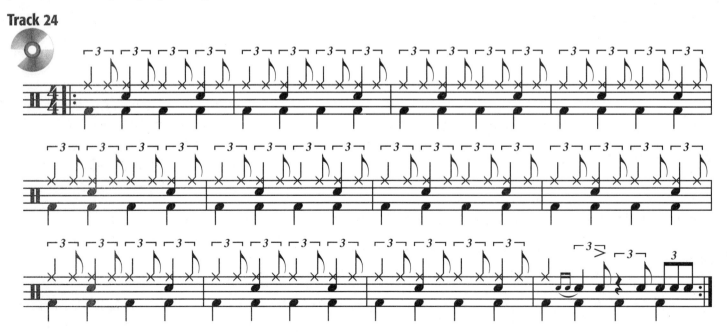

# "Sweet Home Chicago" (ex. 2)
## FROM THE BLUES BROTHERS' *THE BLUES BROTHERS SOUNDTRACK* (1980)

This tune features a nice big drum fill that sets up and kicks in the solo section of the song. Go ahead and try playing the entire one-bar fill, and end it by simultaneously hitting the kick and crash on beat 1 of the following measure.

**Original transcription (3:09):**

Now, try playing the fill within the context of the beat.

# "Stone Crazy"
## FROM BUDDY GUY'S *BUDDY'S BLUES* (1997, SINGLE ORIGINALLY RELEASED IN 1962)

Fred Below uses some perfectly placed double-stroke rolls to make this drum fill flow through the music so nicely. Each roll in this example is a *9-stroke roll*, meaning the surface is struck nine times throughout the course of the roll. The first 9-stroke roll starts with the right stick on beat 8 and carries through until the ride is struck with the right stick on beat 10. The actual sticking is RR–LL–RR–LL–R, with all hits played on the snare drum except for the final right hand hit, which is played on the ride cymbal. The second roll mimics the phrasing of the first and starts on beat 11, and carries through until the ride is struck on beat 1 of the following measure. Go ahead and try playing the fill, and pay attention to keeping the rolls nice and even.

**Original transcription (0:55):**

### The Double-Stroke Roll

Earlier, we learned the "snap, bounce, catch" technique for playing patterns on the ride cymbal. That same technique is used to play drum rolls. To play a double-stroke roll, each stick alternates between this "snap, bounce, catch" motion to create two hits on the drum. Start playing this slowly, using the sticking RR–LL–RR–LL–RR–LL–RR–LL–RR–LL–RR–LL, and so on. Once you get comfortable playing two consecutive hits with each stick and alternating between your left and right hands, begin to speed this exercise up paying close attention to making the notes sound as evenly spaced as possible. When done perfectly, it's hard to tell you are alternating hands or bouncing your sticks, because each drum hit should sound the same. When notated, double-stroke rolls look like this:

Now try playing the fill in the context of the drum beat. Practice until you can play the entire phrase smoothly and comfortably.

# "Pride and Joy"
## FROM STEVIE RAY VAUGHAN AND DOUBLE TROUBLE'S *TEXAS FLOOD* (1983)

Chris Layton plays *stop time* on this tune, which is quite common for the genre and found in hundreds of 12-bar blues songs. The stops start in bar 1 and continue to a triplet build on bar 4. This example begins on bar 12 of a 12-bar blues section, continues with the four measures of stop time, and concludes by leading-in to bar 5 of the 12-bar blues section.

**Original transcription (1:16):**

Let's begin by isolating and playing the short fill that starts on bar 12 of the 12-bar blues section.

Now, let's isolate and repeat the fills that happen on bars 1 and 2 of the stop time section.

Next, let's play bars 3 and 4 of the stop time section and end with a simultaneous kick and ride hit on beat 1 of the following measure.

Finally, put all the examples together, and play stop time just like Chris Layton plays it on "Pride and Joy" and thousands of other drummers play it in their blues bands all the time!

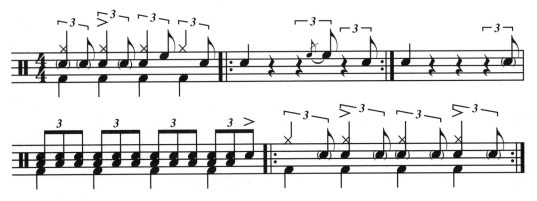

# "Red House" (ex. 1)

## FROM THE JIMI HENDRIX EXPERIENCE'S *ARE YOU EXPERIENCED* (1997 REMASTERED VERSION)

Mitch Mitchell plays a one-bar fill that alternates masterfully between both his hands on the toms and snare, and his foot on the kick drum.

**Original transcription (0:13):**

Let's begin by removing the flams from the fill and playing this pattern that alternates between simultaneous hits on the snare drum and floor tom, and the kick drum played with your foot. Notice that beats 10 and 11 are played consecutively on the snare and floor tom, and beats 12 and 1 of the following measure are played consecutively on the kick with a big crash hit also occurring on beat 1 of the following measure.

Now, let's move the hands around the drums so the fill sounds just like Mitch Mitchell played it on the recording. Your left hand will hit the snare drum on beats 2, 4, 6, and 8, while your right hand moves from the flam played on the snare on beat 2 to the high tom on beat 4, to the floor tom on beat 6, and back to a flam on the snare on beat 8. Beat 10 is played by simultaneously hitting the high tom and floor tom, and beat 11 is played by simultaneously hitting the two floor toms. If you don't have a second floor tom, substitute a rack tom for this hit. The fill concludes with a kick drum hit on beat 12 and a simultaneous kick and crash hit on beat 1 of the following measure. Go ahead and give it a try!

Finally, try playing the fill and then immediately follow it with the drum beat just like Mitch Mitchell played on the recording.

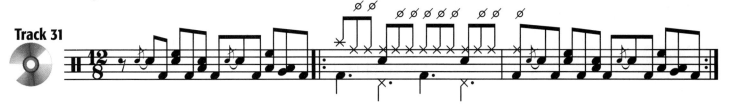

### Improvisation

*Improvisation* means making up the music you're playing as you go along. Instead of playing predetermined beats and fills, improvisation is a totally spontaneous type of music where you can play anything that comes to your mind.

### The Fermata

A *fermata* is used to indicate that a note should be sustained longer than its note value. A fermata is typically used at the end of a piece of music, and the musician holds the note as long as necessary. The length of a fermata is subjective and usually determined by the musician, or the conductor, depending on the musical setting. A fermata looks like this:

# "Red House" (ex. 2)
## FROM THE JIMI HENDRIX EXPERIENCE'S *ARE YOU EXPERIENCED* (1997 REMASTERED VERSION)

This tune features a great drum fill that helps the entire band end the song. This is a fairly typical ending you'll hear in many blues tunes, so once you learn to play it here, you'll be able to apply it, and similar fills, to the end of a wide variety of blues songs. Go ahead and try playing the complete fill as notated below. After you hit the simultaneous kick and crash hits on beats 4 and 7 of the third measure below, go crazy and play any kind of fill you want until you're ready to hit the final note and end the song. This is a place where you can improvise. Give it a try, and have fun with it!

**Original transcription (3:32):**

Among the most respected drummers of the big band era, Irv Cottler recorded with Louis Armstrong, Bing Crosby, Sammy Davis, Jr., Dean Martin, Mel Tormé, and Ella Fitzgerald, among others, but it was with Frank Sinatra that Cottler made his biggest mark. Cottler played with Sinatra for over 30 years, and together they released some of the most beloved songs in history.

# "Everybody Loves Somebody"
## FROM DEAN MARTIN'S *DREAM WITH DEAN* (1964)

Drummer Irv Cottler plays a simple jazz groove on this famous song made popular by Dean Martin in 1964. This basic triplet groove is played in $\frac{4}{4}$ time at a moderate tempo. It's played very similarly to some of the blues grooves learned earlier in this book, so, for the most part, this should be a review of what you already know, only set to jazz instead of blues.

**Original transcription (0:11):**

 **Track 33**

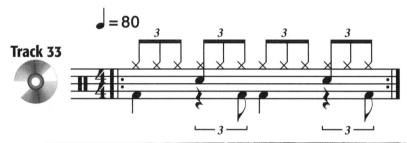

### The Rim Click

The *rim click* is a technique where the tip of the stick is placed on the drumhead near one side of the rim while the butt end of the stick is struck down against the rim on the opposite side. The resulting sound is a sharp high-pitched click.

When notated, a rim click looks like this:

# "What a Wonderful World"
## FROM LOUIE ARMSTRONG'S *ALL TIME GREATEST HITS* (SONG ORIGINALLY RECORDED IN 1968)

Grady Tate's drum beat in this famous Louie Armstrong song is similar to the beat we just played on "Everybody Loves Somebody," except in "What a Wonderful World," the tempo is slower, the middle beat of each triplet on the ride cymbal is removed, and a rim click is played on beats 2 and 4.

**Original transcription (Intro):**

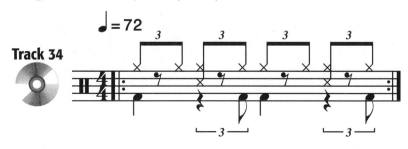

# "I've Got You Under My Skin"
## FROM MICHAEL BUBLÉ'S *IT'S TIME* (2005)

Drummer Jeff Hamilton demonstrates a classic and incredibly versatile swing beat in Michael Bublé's rendition of the Cole Porter original "I've Got You Under My Skin." In this classic beat, the kick drum is played softly on beats 1, 2, 3, and 4; the hi-hat is played with the left foot on beats 2 and 4; a rim click is played on beats 2 and 4; and the ride cymbal is played on beats 1, 2, 3, and 4, and on the "&" of beats 2 and 4. This is a very important drum beat to master because it will work well in most jazz tunes. Start slowly, and gradually increase the tempo as you feel comfortable.

**Original transcription (1:12):**

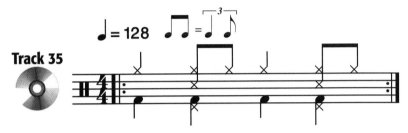

Although the ride cymbal is notated with eighth notes, it's meant to be swung, that is, the groove is intended to be played with a bouncy "swinging" feel instead of a "straight" rock feel. This is usually indicated by inserting the word "swung" at the beginning of the drum notation, or by adding a small notation like this:

It's very common to see jazz songs notated this way, especially when tempos are above 100 bpm, because it's easier to read and write. All the following notations describe the same basic jazz ride cymbal pattern, but we'll focus on the notation style "D" in this book for swing beats over 100 bpm.

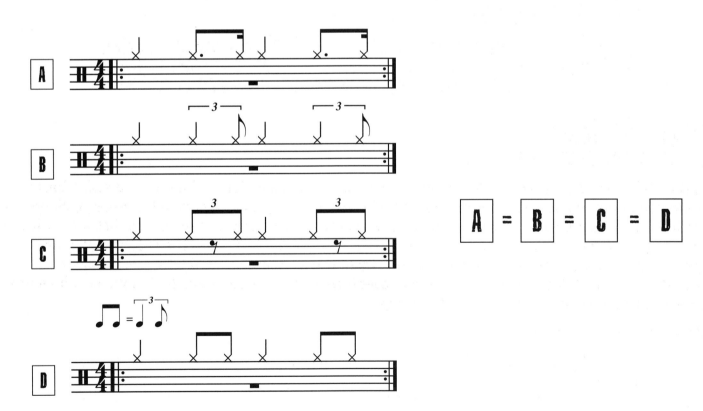

# "Theme from New York, New York"
## FROM FRANK SINATRA'S *TRILOGY: PAST PRESENT AND FUTURE* (1980)

Irv Cottler takes the basic swing beat learned in the previous lesson and modifies it to more closely fit the "vibe" of what the other instruments are playing on this iconic tune. Cottler plays the hi-hat (slightly open) instead of the ride cymbal, the kick on beats 1 and 3, the snare on beats 2 and 4, and the crash cymbal on beat 2. Go ahead and give it a try!

**Original transcription (0:01):**

Track 36

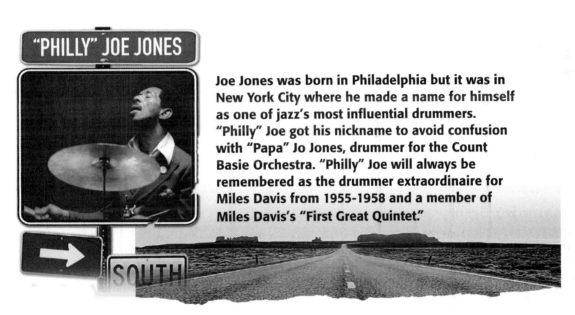

**"PHILLY" JOE JONES**

Joe Jones was born in Philadelphia but it was in New York City where he made a name for himself as one of jazz's most influential drummers. "Philly" Joe got his nickname to avoid confusion with "Papa" Jo Jones, drummer for the Count Basie Orchestra. "Philly" Joe will always be remembered as the drummer extraordinaire for Miles Davis from 1955-1958 and a member of Miles Davis's "First Great Quintet."

# "Straight, No Chaser"
## FROM MILES DAVIS'S *MILESTONES* (1958)

Miles Davis's "go-to" drummer, "Philly" Joe Jones, plays another adaptation of the standard swing beat in this rendition of the jazz standard composed by Thelonious Monk. The drum beat in this excerpt, played under Red Garland's gorgeous piano solo, features a typical swing pattern on the ride cymbal, a rim click on beat 4, and the hi-hat that's played with the left foot on beats 2 and 4. This tune is played at a brisk tempo that may be too challenging at first, so don't try to play it at this tempo right away. Be sure to practice slowly, and gradually increase the tempo over time as you feel comfortable. Eventually, with some practice, you'll be able to play the beat at this tempo.

**Original transcription (6:10):**

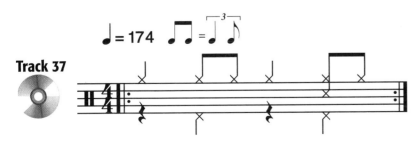

Track 37

# "In a Mellow Tone"
## FROM DUKE ELLINGTON'S *BEST OF DUKE ELLINGTON* (SONG ORIGINALLY RECORDED IN 1939)

Sonny Greer, drummer on Duke Ellington's earliest recordings, plays a very versatile and useful jazz beat on this popular jazz standard. Greer plays a rim click on beats 2 and 4 and a standard swing beat on the hi-hat, but what makes this beat so interesting is that the hi-hat is opened on beats 1 and 3 and closed on beats 2 and 4. This adds an interesting sonic texture to the swing beat. Go ahead and give it a try! Start slowly at first, and gradually increase the tempo as you feel comfortable.

**Original transcription (0:12):**

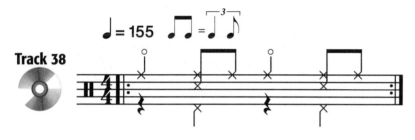

Track 38

# "In the Mood"
## FROM THE GLENN MILLER ORCHESTRA'S *BEST OF GLENN MILLER* (SONG ORIGINALLY RECORDED IN 1939)

Drummer Ray McKinley plays a similar beat on "In the Mood" to the beat we just learned from "In a Mellow Tone." In this tune, the open/closed hi-hat swing pattern remains the same, but the kick is played softly on beats 1, 2, 3, and 4, and there are no rim clicks. Go ahead and try playing the beat slowly, and then gradually increase the tempo until you can play it up to speed.

**Original transcription (0:12):**

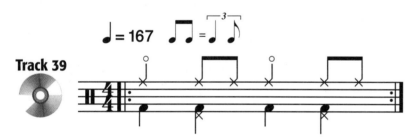

Track 39

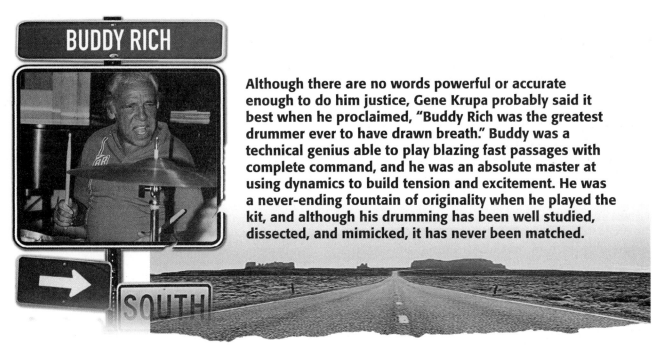

Although there are no words powerful or accurate enough to do him justice, Gene Krupa probably said it best when he proclaimed, "Buddy Rich was the greatest drummer ever to have drawn breath." Buddy was a technical genius able to play blazing fast passages with complete command, and he was an absolute master at using dynamics to build tension and excitement. He was a never-ending fountain of originality when he played the kit, and although his drumming has been well studied, dissected, and mimicked, it has never been matched.

# "Chelsea Bridge"
## FROM BUDDY RICH'S *THE BEST OF BUDDY RICH (PACIFIC JAZZ)* (1997, SONG ORIGINALLY RECORDED IN 1970)

Buddy Rich is praised by drummers around the world because of his amazing control, speed, and musicality. Buddy didn't always play blazing fast notes whenever he sat behind the drum kit; he knew when to play fast and hard, and when to play slow and soft. This excerpt shows off Buddy's slower, softer musical side.

**Original transcription (Intro):**

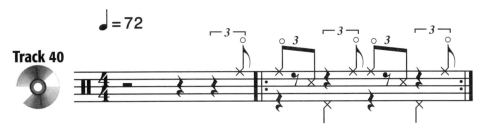

Let's start by playing the open hi-hat with your right stick on beats 1 and 3, and on the third note of each triplet on beats 2 and 4, while closing the hi-hat on beats 2 and 4 with your left foot.

Now, let's play the same beat as in the previous lesson, but this time, let's add a rim click on the third note of each triplet on beats 1 and 3. With a little practice, you'll be playing the groove just like Buddy Rich!

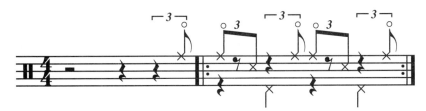

# "Blues Walk"
## FROM LOU DONALDSON'S *BLUES WALK* (1958)

The excerpt in this lesson is an adaptation that combines the drumset part, played by Dave Bailey, and the conga part, played by Ray Barretto, into a beat that a single drummer can play on the drumset. The standard swing pattern is played with the right hand on the ride cymbal, the hi-hat is played with the left foot on beats 2 and 4, the rim click is played on the snare on beat 2, and the high tom is played with the left hand on beat 4 and on the "&" of beat 4. It will take a little practice to switch back and forth between playing the rim click and regular hits on the drum, so start slowly, and stick with it!

**Original transcription (0:01):**

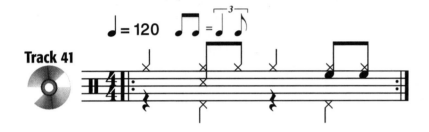

### Syncopation

*Syncopation* refers to unexpected rhythms that occur within a groove. Drummers often play lots of syncopated beats in jazz and funk tunes. Jazz drummers often add syncopated hits with their left hand on the snare drum while they "keep time" with a basic swing pattern on the ride cymbal. These syncopated snare hits often vary constantly throughout the song.

# "The Sidewinder"
## FROM LEE MORGAN'S *THE SIDEWINDER* (1964)

Drummer Billy Higgins plays a catchy swing beat on this tune. Notice how the snare pattern perfectly complements what the piano player is doing. This syncopated drum beat takes coordination, and coordination takes practice, so start by playing each lesson very slowly, and increase the tempo as you feel comfortable.

**Original transcription (0:01):**

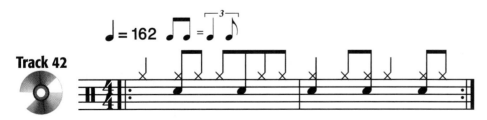

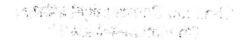

Let's start by playing a basic swing pattern on the ride cymbal, and playing the snare on beat 2 of the first measure and on beat 4 of the second measure.

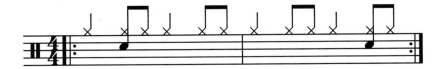

Now, let's play the same beat, but this time, add a snare hit on beat 1 of the second measure.

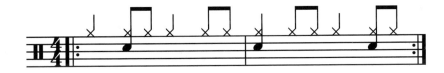

Next, play the same beat, but this time, add another snare hit on the "&" of beat 2 in the second measure.

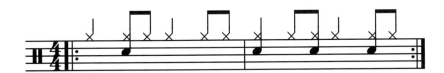

Finally, add one more snare hit, this time on the "&" of beat 3 in the first measure, and you'll be playing the jazz groove just like Billy Higgins plays it on the recording!

Charlotte Community Library
Charlotte MI 48813

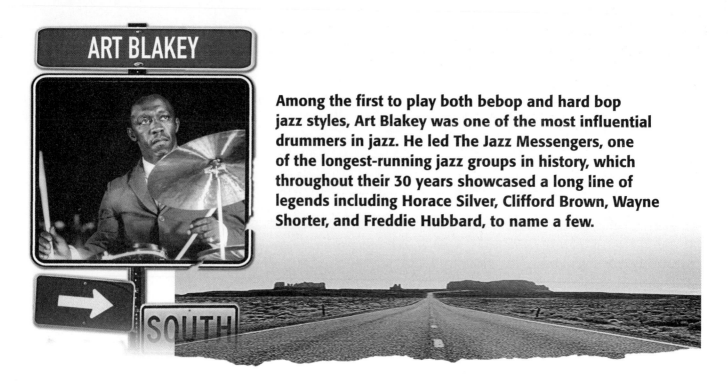

ART BLAKEY

Among the first to play both bebop and hard bop jazz styles, Art Blakey was one of the most influential drummers in jazz. He led The Jazz Messengers, one of the longest-running jazz groups in history, which throughout their 30 years showcased a long line of legends including Horace Silver, Clifford Brown, Wayne Shorter, and Freddie Hubbard, to name a few.

# "Moanin'"
## FROM ART BLAKEY & THE JAZZ MESSENGERS' *MOANIN'* (1958)

Art Blakey led the highly influential Jazz Messengers for over 30 years. This tune features some beautiful playing by Blakey. Notice how he punctuates the music by sometimes adding soft ghosted snare hits right before the backbeat. This is the touch of a master drummer and a skill that's definitely worth learning.

**Original transcription (0:30):**

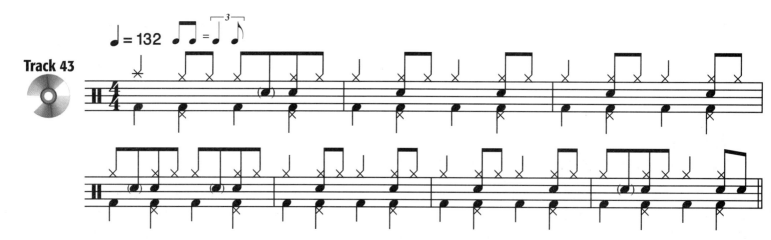

Let's start by playing a basic swing groove with the right hand on the ride, the snare on beats 2 and 4, the kick drum softly on beats 1, 2, 3, and 4 with the right foot, and the hi-hat on beats 2 and 4 with the left foot.

Next, let's play the same beat, but this time, also play a very soft ghost note on the "&" of beat 3. It will take some practice to play a soft ghosted note on the snare immediately followed by a louder hit on the drum, but stick with it. Practice slowly at first, and gradually increase the tempo as you feel comfortable.

Now, let's play the same beat as in the previous lesson, but add another ghosted snare hit on the "&" of beat 1.

Finally, play the full seven-bar excerpt, which has the ghosted snare hits tastefully placed throughout.

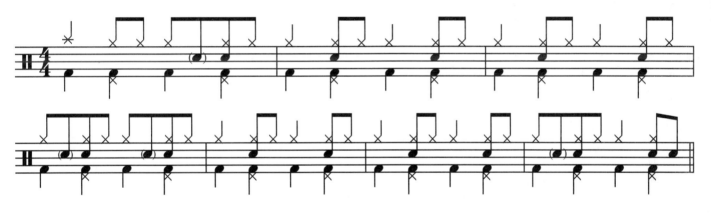

# "So What"
## FROM MILES DAVIS'S *KIND OF BLUE* (1959)

Many jazz drummers embellish the basic swing beat by adding hits that "color" and "texture" the groove. Drummer Jimmy Cobb plays the standard swing beat with a brush in his right hand on the ride cymbal and the hi-hat with his left foot on beats 2 and 4, and he embellishes the groove by playing the kick drum on beat 3 and on the "&" of beat 4—right in tandem with Miles's trumpet. Go ahead and play the beat just like Jimmy Cobb plays on the recording!

**Original transcription (0:52):**

**Track 44**

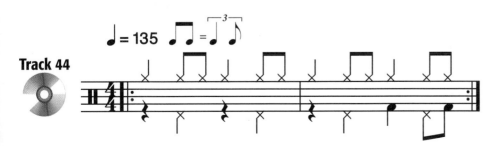

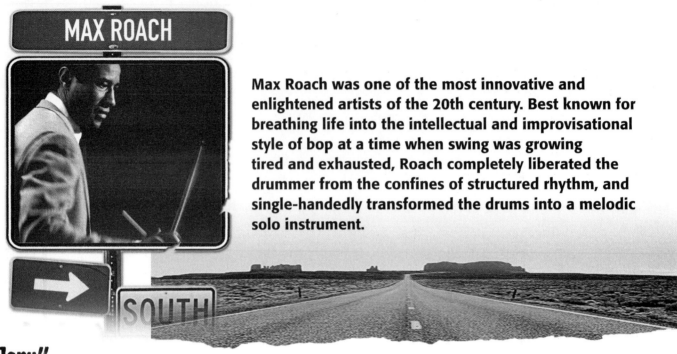

**Max Roach was one of the most innovative and enlightened artists of the 20th century. Best known for breathing life into the intellectual and improvisational style of bop at a time when swing was growing tired and exhausted, Roach completely liberated the drummer from the confines of structured rhythm, and single-handedly transformed the drums into a melodic solo instrument.**

# "Jeru"
## FROM MILES DAVIS'S *BIRTH OF THE COOL* (1949)

Max Roach was one of the most creative and musically tasteful jazz drummers of all time. On this tune, Max hits all the stops on the snare and kick in perfect sync with the band while adding some very tasteful swing beats on the ride cymbal throughout.

**Original transcription (1:30):**

Let's start by isolating and repeating the second measure of the excerpt. This exercise demonstrates that a swing beat doesn't always have to be "ding–ding–da-ding–ding–da-ding." You can play all sorts of variations on that basic swing pattern, like the one written here. Give it a try. Start slowly at first, and gradually increase the tempo as you feel comfortable.

Now, let's isolate and repeat the third measure of the excerpt. This demonstrates another variation on the basic swing pattern we've learned.

Next, let's focus on the fourth measure of the excerpt. This example adds the basic swing pattern as well as the three hits that are played simultaneously on the kick and snare. Playing the exercise with the basic swing pattern will help you see where the kick and snare hits are supposed to be played.
Go ahead and give it a try.

Now, let's play the previous beat, but this time, we'll remove the ride cymbal. Notice that the snare and kick hits are played in the exact same places as in the previous lesson.

Finally, let's put it all together and play the excerpt just like the legendary Max Roach plays it on the recording.

# "In Walked Bud"
## FROM THELONIOUS MONK'S *THE VERY BEST* (2005, SONG ORIGINALLY RELEASED IN 1947)

This fill, played on this tune by Art Blakey, is one of the simplest and most common drum fills you'll find in jazz music. It's incredibly versatile and useful at any tempo, and once you learn this fill, you'll be playing it in jazz songs for the rest of your life. Go ahead and give it a try.

**Original transcription (0:24):**

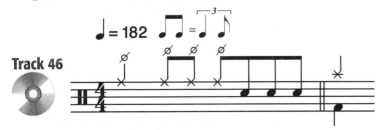

**Track 46**

Let's place the fill at the end of a four-bar phrase and practice repeating blocks of four bars of "time" that the fill connects together. Playing time can be any jazz beat you'd like; you choose the swing beat you want to play, and the tempo. The point of this exercise is to show that you can use this simple fill to connect any two passages of jazz music rather effortlessly, even in a swing beat you just made up!

You'll see in this example that there are three bars with four slashes in each. This is music notation shorthand used to indicate playing time. When you see this, play any groove you'd like that's appropriate to the time feel.

**Track 47**

# "I've Got You Under My Skin" (ex. 1)
## FROM MICHAEL BUBLÉ'S *IT'S TIME* (2005)

This is a second "universal" drum fill that works in nearly any jazz fill application. It's very similar to the previous drum fill, but Jeff Hamilton plays a drag on beat 4 instead of a snare hit on the "&" of beat 3. Go ahead and try playing this versatile drum fill.

**Original transcription (1:59):**

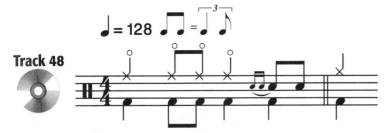

**Track 48**

Now, like in the previous lesson, let's improvise a swing beat—anything you'd like to play, and at any tempo you wish—and connect four-bar phrases with this simple drum fill.

**Track 49**

JEFF HAMILTON

Praised for his originality, creativity, sensitivity, dynamics, feel, and musical maturity, Jeff Hamilton is as in-demand as jazz drummers get. Jeff has played the drums on nearly 200 recordings from artists including Natalie Cole, Diana Krall, Oscar Peterson, Barney Kessel, and Ray Brown, to name a few.

# "I've Got You Under My Skin" (ex. 2)
## FROM MICHAEL BUBLÉ'S *IT'S TIME* (2005)

In this fill, Jeff Hamilton plays strategically placed snare hits to accent the phrase in the horn section. This is a very useful concept drummers employ to give a song more excitement and add pronunciation to certain key phrases.

**Original transcription (1:24):**

Track 50

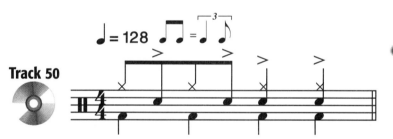

### Cues

*Cues* are small notes used in drum charts to communicate a melodic line that is played by another instrument, or several instruments, in the band. The drummer can insert a short fill to set up the band to play the melodic line, or the drummer can play the rhythm along with the other instrument(s) to give the melodic phrase even more impact.

Sometimes you'll see the types of phrases described above written as a cue on a drum chart, like in this example.

Track 51

# "I've Got You Under My Skin" (ex. 3)
## FROM MICHAEL BUBLÉ'S *IT'S TIME* (2005)

So far, all the drum fills we've explored are played on the snare drum. Fills can also be played all around the drumset. In this excerpt, Jeff Hamilton incorporates the snare, rack tom, kick drum, and hi-hat into his drum fill. Go ahead and give it a try. Start slowly at first, and gradually increase the tempo as you feel comfortable.

**Original transcription (1:51):**

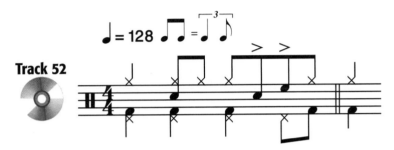

Now, let's practice playing this fill within the context of the beat. In this exercise, we'll play the fill at the end of a repeating four-bar phrase.

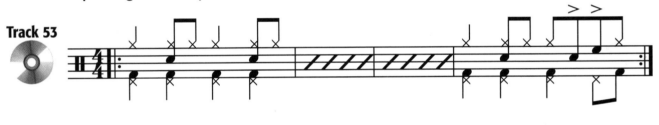

# "Theme from New York, New York"
## FROM FRANK SINATRA'S *TRILOGY: PAST PRESENT AND FUTURE* (1980)

Irv Cottler plays a dramatic, yet simple, triplet pattern fill on the snare and floor tom to increase the intensity in this section of the song. In this example, the snare and floor tom are played in unison, with the snare played with the left hand and the floor tom played with the right hand.

**Original transcription (1:50):**

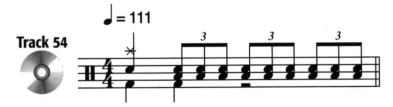

This is a very common fill, especially on jazz tunes played at slow to moderate tempos. Here's an alternative way of playing the fill that adds even more intensity by playing the kick drum on all four beats.

### The Multiple Bounce Roll (Press Roll, Buzz Roll)

The *multiple bounce roll,* sometimes called a *press roll* or a *buzz roll,* is one of the 40 international drum rudiments. It's played by pressing the sticks into the head in an alternating pattern to create the audible effect of a buzzing, white noise, type of sound. When notated, multiple bounce rolls look like this:

### Crescendo and Decrescendo

*Crescendo* indicates that the volume is gradually increasing. *Decrescendo* indicates that the volume is gradually decreasing. When notated, a crescendo looks like this:

and a decrescendo looks like this:

# "Moanin'"
## FROM ART BLAKEY & THE JAZZ MESSENGERS' *MOANIN'* (1958)

The multiple bounce roll is another key tool in the jazz drummer's arsenal that can be used as a drum fill to bridge two sections of a song. Art Blakey starts the roll softly in the beginning and gradually crescendos throughout the measure until he hits the crash and kick on beat 1 of the following measure.

**Original transcription (0:58):**

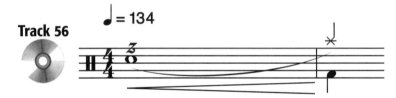

You could also play the press roll with a decrescendo. Let's practice playing with dynamics on this four-bar phrase.

Now, let's try it with the dynamic markings reversed. In this exercise, the press roll is played with a crescendo, and the swing beat is played with a decrescendo. Go ahead and give it a try.

## "In Walked Bud"
### FROM THELONIOUS MONK'S *THE VERY BEST* (2005, SONG ORIGINALLY RELEASED IN 1947)

Art Blakey plays a great one-bar drum fill that starts on the snare and finishes on the kick. Notice how Blakey's use of straight (not swung) eighth notes and a sixteenth-note figure really stands out and punctuates the music. Go ahead and give it a try.

**Original transcription (2:07):**

Now, let's practice playing the fill within the context of a swing beat.

## "Everybody Loves Somebody" (ex. 1)
### FROM DEAN MARTIN'S *DREAM WITH DEAN* (1964)

Irv Cottler showcases some quick, yet delicate, left hand playing on the snare in this smooth drum fill. The three consecutive snare hits ending with the accent on beat 4 are a little tricky and take some practice to play smoothly, so start slowly, and gradually increase the tempo as you feel comfortable.

**Original transcription (0:30):**

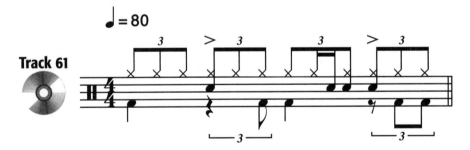

Now, try playing it within the context of the beat.

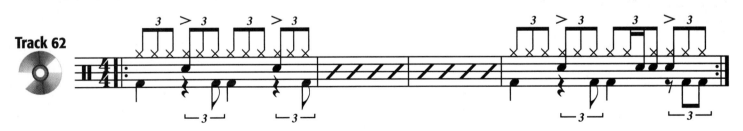

# "Everybody Loves Somebody" (ex. 2)
## FROM DEAN MARTIN'S *DREAM WITH DEAN* (1964)

Here's another beautiful drum fill played by Irv Cottler. In this excerpt, Cottler adds several snare hits throughout the drum fill while maintaining the continuity of the beat with the ride cymbal.

**Original transcription (0:54):**

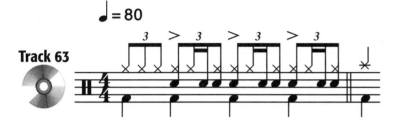

**Track 63**

Let's start by playing and repeating this simplified version of the fill. Play triplets on the ride cymbal with your right hand, the snare drum on beats 2 and 4 with your left hand, and the kick on beats 1, 2, 3, and 4. Hit the snare with your left stick in the space between the second and third notes of the triplet that starts on beat 4, immediately followed by another snare hit with your left stick on the third note of the triplet. Go ahead and give it a try. Start slowly at first, and gradually increase the tempo as you feel comfortable.

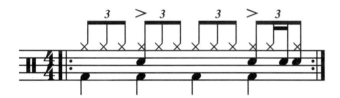

Next, let's add the same pattern starting on beat 2.

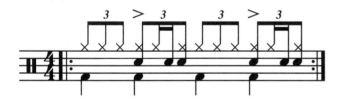

Finally, add the same pattern to beat 3, and with a little practice, you'll be playing the drum fill just like Irv Cottler plays it on the recording.

# Congratulations!

You have completed **Level 2** of the *On the Beaten Path: Beginning Drumset Course.* **Level 3** explores **authentic** country, funk, reggae, and Latin beats, in addition to more authentic jazz beats and jazz fills. **Plus,** you'll learn about first and second endings, polyrhythms, sextuplets, dropping bombs, rim shots, open hi-hat splashes, stick clicks, the 5-stroke roll, trading fours, and buzz strokes. You'll also learn to play in more time signatures, and to play with time/meter/tempo manipulations like double time, half time, ritardandos, and accelerandos. So, what are you waiting for? Let's get started on **Level 3!**

*Audio examples performed by Rich Lackowski.*
*Instructional photos by Larry Lytle.*

# "On the Road Again"
## FROM WILLIE NELSON'S *16 BIGGEST HITS* (1998, ORIGINALLY RELEASED ON THE *HONEYSUCKLE ROSE* SOUNDTRACK IN 1980)

"On the Road Again" is one of the most popular country songs of all time. Drummer Paul English, who has played with Nelson since 1955, lays down a standard country "train beat" by playing an accented two-handed pattern on the snare and playing the kick drum on beats 1 and 3.

**Original transcription (0:25):**

Let's start by playing the standard train beat. This groove is slightly swung, which means it's not played with ultra-precise eighth notes, and it's also not quite swung like a swing beat. Instead, it falls somewhere in the middle of these two extremes. Play the kick on beats 1 and 3 while playing continuous eighth notes on the snare, alternating left and right hands. Be sure to accent beats 2 and 4. Go ahead and give it a try.

Sometimes drummers add an extra accent in the train beat, just to give it a slight variation, which keeps it interesting.

Another common variation in the train beat is adding an additional accent to the "&" of beat 1 or, in this exercise, to the "&" of beat 3.

**First and second endings**

First and second endings are used in music notation when a section of music is played the same all the way through except for the ending. Instead of writing the music out twice with only the ending of the section changing, the use of first and second endings make it easier to notate and easier for the musician to read.

# "The Devil Went Down to Georgia"
## FROM THE CHARLIE DANIELS BAND'S *MILLION MILE REFLECTIONS* (1979)

Similar in feel to "On the Road Again" but much faster, this is a good example of a *train beat*, competently played by drummer James Marshall. This lesson features an eight bar excerpt and is notated using first and second endings. When you get to the repeat sign (first ending), go back to the opposite facing repeat sign which, in this case, is at the beginning of the transcription. When you finish playing the third measure the second time, skip the first ending and jump straight to the second ending, which adds an accent on the "&" of beat 3. Go ahead and give it a try!

**Track 4**

**Original transcription (0:21):**

## BASIC FUNK BEATS

# "Groovy Lady"
## FROM THE METERS' *FUNKIFY YOUR LIFE: THE METERS ANTHOLOGY* (1995)

Joseph "Zigaboo" Modeliste is one of the funkiest drummers on the planet. If you would like to play funk music, do yourself a favor and buy this album. It's loaded with some of the best funk drumming ever played, as demonstrated in this excerpt from "Groovy Lady."

**Original transcription (Intro):**

**Track 5**

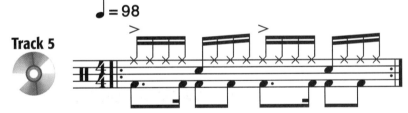

Let's start by playing sixteenth notes on the hi-hat by alternating each stick, starting with your right hand. Hit the snare on beats 2 and 4 with your right hand. Play the kick on beats 1 and 3, on the "&" of beats 2 and 4, and on the "ah" of beats 1 and 3.

Now, add in the accents on beats 1 and 3, and the additional kick drum hits on beats 2 and 4 and you'll be playing the funky beat just like Zigaboo plays it on the recording!

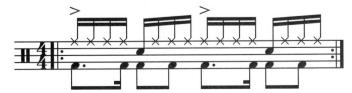

# "Doodle Loop (The World is a Little Bit Under the Weather)"
## FROM THE METERS' *FUNKIFY YOUR LIFE: THE METERS ANTHOLOGY* (1995)

This tune also features some funky playing by Zigaboo Modeliste and showcases some of his beautifully syncopated kick drum playing.

**Original transcription (Intro):**

Let's start by playing eighth notes on the hi-hat, the snare on beats 2 and 4, and the kick drum on beats 1 and 3, and on the "&" of beats 2 and 4.

Now, let's play the same groove as in the previous lesson, only this time, we'll add kick drum hits on the "ah" of beats 1 and 3.

Finally, play the same groove as in the previous lesson, but this time, remove the kick drum hit on beat 3. Start slowly and gradually increase the tempo as you feel comfortable.

Widely acknowledged as the innovator of second-line funk playing, Zigaboo Modeliste is without a doubt one of the most influential, creative, and soulful artists to ever live. This highly acclaimed drummer and New Orleans legend has written and recorded over 200 songs with The Meters, spanning 30 national and international album releases. He's touched many with his incredible playing and will forever be considered the king of funk drumming.

# "Unfunky UFO"
## FROM PARLIAMENT'S *MOTHERSHIP CONNECTION* (1976)

This album is widely accepted as Parliament's best, and is definitely one of the "must-hear" milestones on the beaten path of funk. Parliament was notorious for having a revolving door of members throughout their long career, and four drummers are credited on this album, including bassist Bootsy Collins. So it's a bit unclear as to which drummer played on which songs, but all the drummers—Jerome "Bigfoot" Brailey, Bootsy Collins, Gary "Mudbone" Cooper, and Ramon Tiki Fulwood—are incredibly talented, unbelievably funky, and worth checking out.

**Original transcription (0:22):**

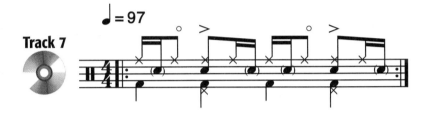

Let's start by playing a simple "four on the floor" beat.

Now, let's add a ghost note on the snare on the "ah" of beats 2 and 4. Pay careful attention to playing the ghost notes at a much quieter volume then the accented snare hits on beats 2 and 4.

Next, let's play the "four on the floor" beat, and this time, let's play a ghost note on the "e" of beats 1 and 3. Again, make sure there is a large contrast in volume between the ghost notes and the accented notes.

Now, let's combine the previous two exercises and play the "four on the floor" beat with accented snare hits on beats 2 and 4, and ghost notes on the "e" of beats 1 and 3, and on the "ah" of beats 2 and 4.

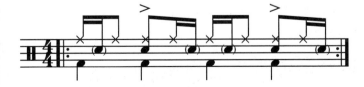

Next, let's play the same beat as in the previous exercise, but this time, let's play it with an open hi-hat on the "&" of each beat by stomping your left foot on the hi-hat pedal on beats 1, 2, 3, and 4.

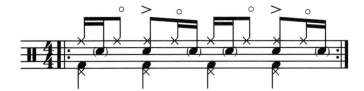

Finally, let's play the same beat as in the previous exercise, but this time, we'll remove the open hi-hat hits on the "&" of beats 2 and 4 by only stomping your foot on the hi-hat pedal on beats 2 and 4.

# "You Can Make It If You Try"
## FROM SLY & THE FAMILY STONES' *STAND!* (1969)

Drummer Greg Errico lays down quite a driving funk groove starting at 0:52 into this song. He achieves this driving feel by playing the snare drum on beats 1, 2, and 4, and by playing a syncopated kick drum pattern.

**Original transcription (0:52):**

**Track 8**

Let's start by playing eighth notes on the hi-hat, the snare on beats 1, 2 and 4, and the kick drum on beat 3 and on the "&" of beat 3.

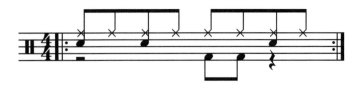

Now, let's add in some additional kick drum hits. You may need to practice this slowly at first and gradually increase the tempo as you feel comfortable.

Finally, add in the last kick drum hit on the "e" of beat 1, and you'll be playing the groove just like Greg Errico plays it on the original recording!

# "Tippi-Toes"
## FROM THE METERS' *STRUTTIN'* (1970)

Zigaboo incorporates syncopated kick drum hits and open hi-hat hits into this gloriously funky groove.

**Original transcription (0:19):**

Track 9

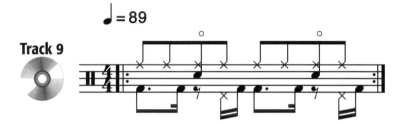

Let's start by playing eighth notes on the hi-hat, the snare on beats 2 and 4, and the kick drum on beats 1 and 3. Lift your left foot off the hi-hat pedal on beats 2 and 4, and stomp your foot back down on the pedal on the "&" of beats 2 and 4.

Next, let's play the same groove as in the previous lesson, but this time, we'll add kick drum hits on the "ah" of beats 1 and 3.

Finally, add kick drum hits on the "ah" of beats 2 and 4 and you'll be playing this ultra funky groove just like Zigaboo plays it on the recording!

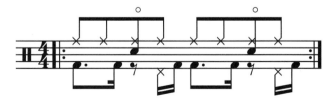

# "Brick House"
## FROM THE COMMODORES' *COMMODORES* (1977)

This is definitely one of the most popular and widely-covered funk tunes ever written. Drummer Walter Orange plays this contagious beat that's been heard by generations of dancers all around the world.

**Original transcription (0:30):**

Let's start by playing this simplified version of the groove. Play eighth notes on the hi-hat, the snare on beats 2 and 4, and the kick on beats 1 and 3, and on the "&" of beats 2 and 4.

Now, let's spice up the beat by opening the hi-hat on the "&" of beat 4 and closing it again on beat 1 of the following measure.

Next, let's add an additional kick hit on the "ah" of beat 3.

Now, let's play the same groove as in the previous lesson, but this time, let's remove the kick drum hit that was played on beat 1.

Finally, put it all together and play the groove just like Walter Orange played it on the recording!

# "Chameleon"
## FROM HERBIE HANCOCK'S *HEAD HUNTERS* (1973)

Drummer Harvey Mason plays a seriously funky groove on this, one of the most popular funk tunes ever written.

**Original transcription (0:16):**

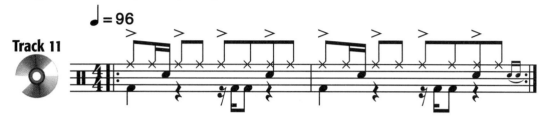

Let's start by playing eighth notes on the hi-hat, kick on beat 1 and on the "&" of beat 3, and the snare on the "ah" of beat 1 and on beat 4. Start slowly at first and gradually increase the tempo as you feel comfortable.

Now, let's play the same groove as in the previous lesson, but this time, we'll add a kick hit on the "e" of beat 3. Go ahead and give it a try.

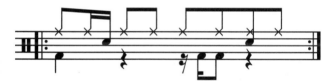

Next, let's play the same groove as in the previous exercise, but this time, we'll add a drag on the snare drum that leads into the kick drum and hi-hat hits on beat 1 of the following measure. Go ahead and give it a try.

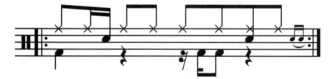

Now, put it all together, add accents on the hi-hat on beats 1, 2, 3, and 4, and you'll be playing the funky groove just like Harvey Mason plays it on the recording!

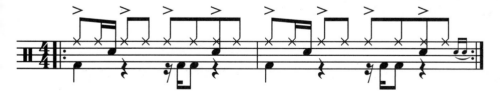

# "Thinking"
## FROM THE METERS' *LOOK-KA PY PY* (1969)

This is another example of Zigaboo's incredibly funky drumming. One thing that makes this beat so fun to play is that the open hi-hat, which begins on beat 4, only lasts for half of one beat. You'll start to hear this concept quite a bit as you listen to more and more funk music.

**Original transcription (0:01):**

Let's start by playing quarter notes on the hi-hat, the snare on beats 2 and 4, and the kick drum on beat 1, and on the "&" and "ah" of beat 3.

Next, let's play the same groove as in the previous exercise, but this time we'll add an open hi-hat on beat 4. For this exercise, let's let that open hi-hat ring out all the way until beat 1 of the following measure, at which point you'll stomp your foot back on the hi-hat pedal. Go ahead and give it a try!

Finally, let's play the same beat, but this time we'll shorten the duration of the open hi-hat that starts on beat 4 to last the duration of an eighth note. To do this, lift your foot off the hi-hat pedal on beat 4, and stomp your foot back down on the pedal on the "&" of beat 4. Practice this slowly and be patient. You can do it!

JOHN JABO STARKS

James Brown, after much persistence, convinced Jabo Starks to leave his gig with the Bobby "Blue" Band and join the James Brown Orchestra in 1965. Jabo recorded the drums on more charting singles than any other drummer in James Brown's extensive career, including "Sex Machine," "Papa Don't Take No Mess," "Make It Funky," "Super Bad," "The Payback," "Doin' It to Death," and "Licking Stick," just to name a few.

# "Super Bad, Pt. 1"
## FROM JAMES BROWN'S *70'S FUNK CLASSICS* (2004, SINGLE ORIGINALLY RELEASED IN 1970)

John "Jabo" Starks plays one of the all-time greatest and funkiest beats ever recorded on this tune. Listen to how Jabo skillfully incorporates his trademark open hi-hat hits on the "&" of beats 1 and 3 while he plays syncopated snare hits and a steady kick drum pattern that glues it all together. Now that's some funky drumming!

**Original transcription (0:02):**

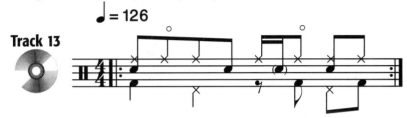

Let's begin by playing eighth notes on the hi-hat, and add in the syncopated snare hits on beat 1, the "&" of beat 2, and on beat 4.

Next, let's add in kick drum hits on beat 1 and the "&" of beats 3 and 4.

Now, add a ghosted snare hit on the "e" of beat 3.

Next, open the hi-hat on the "&" of beat 1 and close it again on beat 2.

Finally, add an additional open hi-hat on the "&" of beat 3 and you'll be playing this super funky beat just like Jabo plays it on the recording.

# "54-46 That's My Number"
## FROM TOOTS & THE MAYTALS' *THE VERY BEST OF TOOTS & THE MAYTALS* (2000, SINGLE ORIGINALLY RELEASED IN 1968)

Drummer Paul Douglas plays a classic one-drop beat on this tune by one of the pioneering bands of reggae music. Play quarter notes on the hi-hat on beats 1, 2, 3 and 4, while playing a rim click and a simultaneous kick drum hit on beat 3. Go ahead and give it a try!

**Original transcription (0:04):**

### One-Drop

The one-drop rhythm is a groove that dominates roots reggae drumming with the kick drum landing on beat 3, or, depending on how the song is counted and notated, on beats 2 and 4 of each measure. The groove got its name from the intentional omission of beat 1 on the kick drum. The "one" is dropped in this popular reggae rhythm.

# "Buffalo Soldier"
## FROM BOB MARLEY AND THE WAILERS' *CONFRONTATION* (1983)

Carlton Barrett plays another type of reggae beat in this tune where the kick is played on beats 1, 2, 3, and 4, and a rim click is played on beat 3 of the first two measures, and on the last note of the triplet that starts on beat 4 in the second measure.

**Original transcription (0:24):**

### One-Measure Repeat

*One-measure repeats* are used to indicate that you should play exactly what was written in the previous measure. When notated, a one-measure repeat looks like this:

# "One Love / People Get Ready"
## FROM BOB MARLEY AND THE WAILERS' *EXODUS* (1977)

Carlton Barrett masterfully incorporates accented notes and a bouncy hi-hat feel on this timeless tune.

**Track 16**

**Original transcription (0:02):**

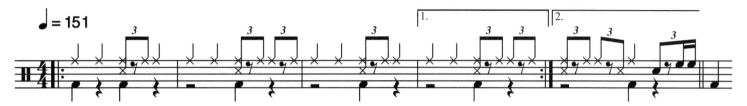

Let's start by playing and repeating a basic one-drop rhythm by hitting the hi-hat on beats 1, 2, 3, and 4, and playing a rim click and a kick drum hit together on beat 3.

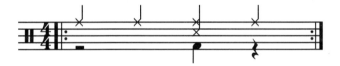

Sometimes, reggae drummers embellish the beat a bit by varying the hits on the hi-hat. The bouncy feel that they achieve is similar to what we learned when playing a swing beat. Start slowly and gradually increase the tempo as you feel comfortable.

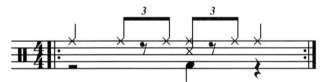

In this next exercise, we'll play a very common reggae drum fill followed by a simple one-drop rhythm. To play the fill, hit a rim click on beat 1 and on the last note of the triplet that starts on beat 2. Then, hit the snare on beat 4 with the snares turned off so it sounds like a high-pitched rack tom or a timbale.

Finally, let's put it all together, adding the rack tom to the fill, and play this one-drop reggae groove just like Carlton Barrett plays it on the recording!

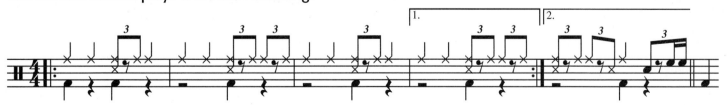

# "Rootsman Skanking"

## FROM BUNNY WAILERS' *ROOTSMAN SKANKING* (1987)

Sly Dunbar, one of the most prolific and important drummers to ever come out of Jamaica, plays this fantastic reggae beat that mixes rim clicks, snare hits, and open hi-hats together to create a groove that perfectly compliments this song.

**Original transcription (0:01):**

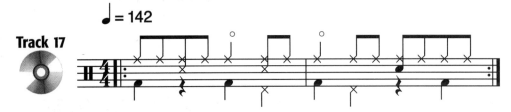

Let's start by playing this simplified version of the groove.

Next, let's play the same beat as in the last exercise, but this time, we'll open the hi-hat on beat 3 of the first measure, and on beat 1 of the second measure.

Now, let's play eighth notes on the hi-hat in the first measure whenever you're not playing an open hi-hat. When you are playing an open hi-hat, let the cymbals ring out for a full quarter note beat.

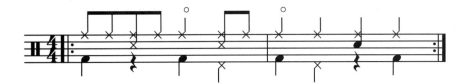

Finally, play eighth notes on the hi-hat in the second measure when you're not playing an open hi-hat. Start slowly and increase the tempo as you feel comfortable.

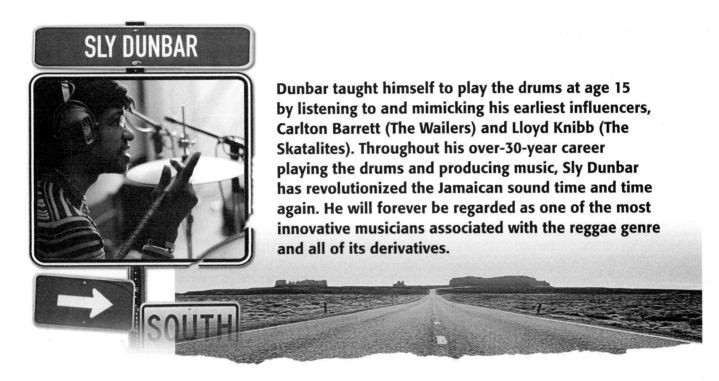

SLY DUNBAR

Dunbar taught himself to play the drums at age 15 by listening to and mimicking his earliest influencers, Carlton Barrett (The Wailers) and Lloyd Knibb (The Skatalites). Throughout his over-30-year career playing the drums and producing music, Sly Dunbar has revolutionized the Jamaican sound time and time again. He will forever be regarded as one of the most innovative musicians associated with the reggae genre and all of its derivatives.

# BASIC LATIN BEATS

## "The Girl from Ipanema"
### FROM ASTRUD GILBERTO, JOÃO GILBERTO, & STAN GETZ'S *GETZ/GILBERTO* (1964)

This is quite possibly the most popular bossa nova tune ever written. Drummer Milton Banana plays a very straight forward groove, primarily on the hi-hat, with a few accents added throughout. Go ahead and try playing along with the groove that's notated here.

**Bossa Nova**

The bossa nova rhythm is a common groove found in Brazilian music.

Original transcription (0:22):

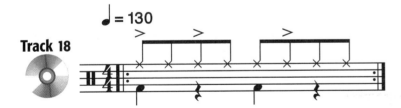

Track 18

This next lesson shows a very common bossa nova groove. Go ahead and try playing this groove along with the tune. The rim clicks are very important, so make sure you pay special attention to hitting them in the right places.

Track 19

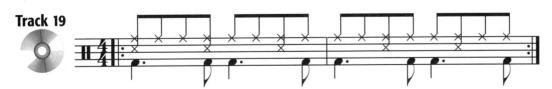

# "Fee"
## FROM PHISH'S *JUNTA* (1989)

The bossa nova beat has found its way into other styles of music. In this tune, drummer Jon Fishman adapts a bossa nova groove into a jam band setting.

**Original transcription (0:15):**

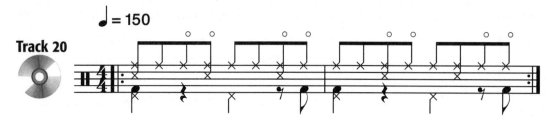

Let's start by playing eighth notes on the hi-hat with your right hand. Press the hi-hat pedal down with your left foot on beats 1 and 3, and raise your left foot off the pedal on beats 2 and 4.

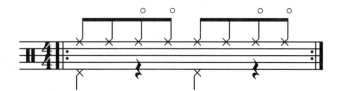

Now, play the same groove as in the previous lesson, but this time, add a rim click on beat 1, the "&" of beat 2, and on beat 4 in the first measure, and on beat 2 and the "&" of beat 3 in the second measure.

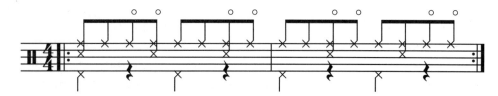

Next, let's play the same groove as in the previous lesson, but this time, let's add a kick drum hit on beat 1 of each measure.

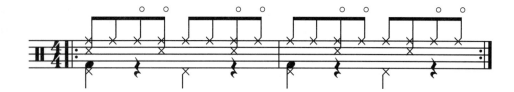

Finally, add another kick drum hit on the "&" of beat 4 in each measure, and you'll be playing the groove just like Jon Fishman plays it on the recording!

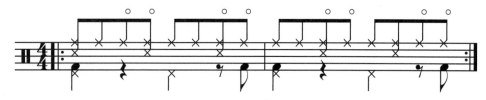

## "Desafinado (Off Key)"
### FROM CHARLIE BYRD & STAN GETZ'S *JAZZ SAMBA* (1962)

Drummers Buddy Deppenschmidt and Bill Reichenbach play an up-tempo bosa nova groove in this famous tune. This transcription and lesson is a drumset adaptation of the original groove that blends together the drum and percussion parts played by Deppenschmidt and Reichenback. An interesting note is that drummer John Densmore took this basic bossa nova groove and played it at a blazing 188 BPM in the song "Break On Through (To the Other Side)" from the Doors's self-titled debut album.

**Original transcription (0:14):**

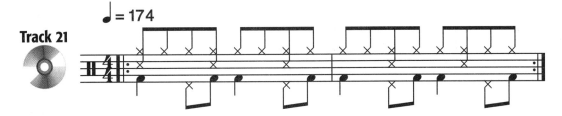

Let's start by playing eighth notes on the ride cymbal, the kick on beats 1 and 3, and on the "&" of beats 2 and 4, and the hi-hat with your foot on beats 2 and 4.

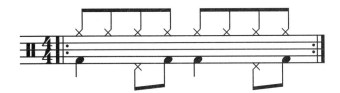

Next, let's play the same groove as in the previous lesson, but this time, we'll add rim clicks on beats 1 and 4 of the first measure, and to beat 2 of the second measure.

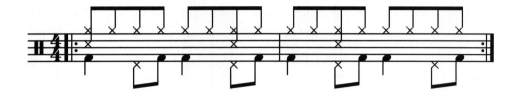

Finally, add in another rim click on the "&" of beat 2 in the first measure, and on the "&" of beat 3 in the second measure and you'll be playing the bossa nova groove! If you play it faster, at 188 BPM, you'll be playing the groove in "Break on Through (To the Other Side)!"

**We learned dozens of jazz beats and fills** in Level 2 of the *On the Beaten Path: Beginning Drumset Course.* Here, in the next two sections of this book, we continue our exploration of this great genre with more jazz beats and jazz fills to round out your drumming skills and to introduce new musical concepts. Enjoy!

### Dropping Bombs

*Dropping bombs* is a term that refers to a drummer placing unexpected kick drum hits within a jazz groove. Dropping bombs is common in bebop-style drumming (a sub-genre of jazz usually characterized by very fast tempos and virtuoso musicians) and was pioneered by drummers Kenny Clarke, Max Roach, and Art Blakey.

# "In Walked Bud"
## FROM THELONIOUS MONK'S *THE VERY BEST* (2005, SONG ORIGINALLY RECORDED IN 1947)

Art Blakey masterfully plays some of his famous bomb drops on this jazz standard, composed by the great Thelonious Monk. This excerpt begins with some bomb drops in the first two measures, and then switches to some syncopated snare hits in the last two measures.

**Track 22    Original transcription (0:24):**

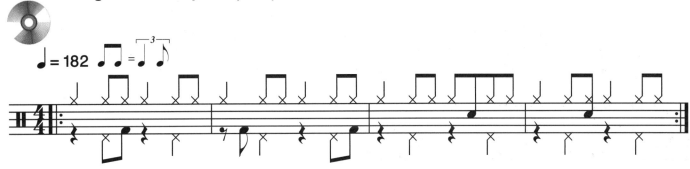

Let's begin by isolating and repeating the first measure of the excerpt. At a slow tempo, play a couple measures of the basic swing pattern on the ride cymbal with your right hand and the hi-hat with your foot. Then starting on measure 3 of this exercise, add in the bomb drop by playing the kick on the "&" of beat 2 and repeat that measure until you can play this comfortably. Gradually increase the tempo as you feel comfortable.

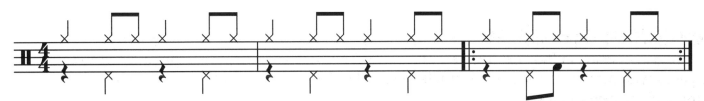

Now, let's isolate and repeat the second measure of the excerpt. This time, the bomb drops occur on the "&" of beats 1 and 4. Like in the previous lesson, we'll begin by playing a couple measures of the traditional swing pattern before proceeding to the bomb drops in measure 3. Go ahead and give it a try, slowly at first, and gradually faster as you feel comfortable.

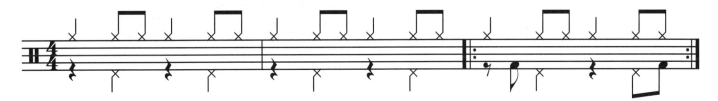

Let's combine what we learned in the previous two lessons and practice playing and repeating the first two measures of the excerpt. Again, we'll start with a couple measures of keeping time before incorporating the bomb drops.

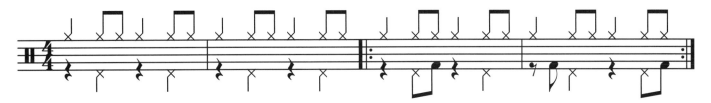

Next, let's isolate and repeat the last two measures of the excerpt. Begin by playing a basic swing pattern for two measures, and starting in measure 3, play the syncopated snare hits with your left hand on the "&" of beat 3, and the "&" of beat 2 in the fourth measure. Start slowly and increase the tempo as you feel comfortable.

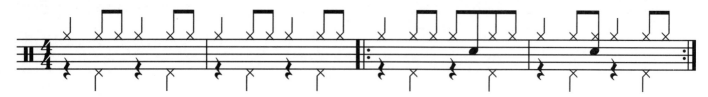

Finally, let's put it all together and play the excerpt complete with bomb drops and syncopated snare hits just like Art Blakey plays it on the recording.

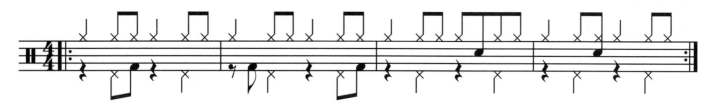

## MORE JAZZ FILLS

# "In Walked Bud" (ex. 1)
## FROM THELONIOUS MONK'S *THE VERY BEST*
## (2005, SONG ORIGINALLY RECORDED IN 1947)

Art Blakey plays some quick snare hits before ending the fill with a quarter-note triplet with his left hand on the snare while playing quarter notes on the ride with his right hand. The result is a "2 against 3" polyrhythm, with two beats played on the ride with the right hand for every three beats played on the snare with the left hand. Go ahead and give the fill a try. Start slowly at first, and gradually increase the speed as you feel comfortable.

**Original transcription (1:48):**

**Polyrhythms**

A *polyrhythm* is a rhythm of one type played against a rhythm of a different type. A common example of a polyrhythm is when you play eighth notes on top of eighth note triplets. There are two eighth notes played for every three eighth notes in a triplet, so this is a "2 against 3" polyrhythm.

**Track 23**

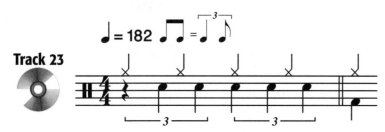

Now, let's practice playing the fill within the context of the beat.

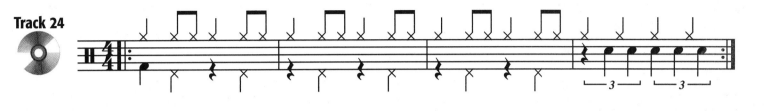

# "In Walked Bud" (ex. 2)

**FROM THELONIOUS MONK'S *THE VERY BEST* (2005, SONG ORIGINALLY RECORDED IN 1947)**
Art Blakey plays a simple, yet elegant, fill in this excerpt with a smooth open roll that starts on beat 3 and continues until beat 1 of the following measure. Notice how smoothly Blakey plays this so the momentum of the groove never stops. Go ahead and give it a try.

**Original transcription (0:44):**

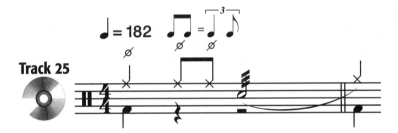

Now, let's practice playing the fill within the context of the beat.

**Rim Shot**

A *rim shot* is played by hitting the tip of the stick on the head of the snare drum while simultaneously hitting the shaft of the stick on the rim of the drum. The resulting sound is a loud, accented, high-pitched, explosive crack.

# "Straight, No Chaser"
## FROM MILES DAVIS'S *MILESTONES* (1958)

It's clear why Miles Davis loved playing with "Philly" Joe Jones. Listen to how effortless, yet complex, Jones's playing is. "Philly" Joe had a gift to which we mortal drummers all aspire. This excerpt showcases some very tasty left hand snare work in the first measure, followed by a quick sixteenth-note fill starting on the "&" of beat 1 in the second measure that continues until slamming a rim shot down on beat 3, and finishing with some simultaneous ride and kick hits.

**Original transcription (9:23):**

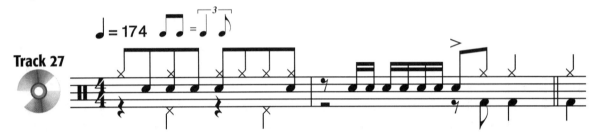

Let's start by isolating and repeating the first measure of the fill. There are a lot of snare embellishments played with the left hand in this part of the fill, so start slowly, and gradually increase the tempo as you feel comfortable.

Now, let's play and repeat the following two-bar example. The first measure is fairly simple, and it sets up the simultaneous hit on the snare and the ride on the "&" of beat 4 so you are ready to play the second measure of the fill. At the end of the string of sixteenth notes played in the second measure, hit a nice, strong rim shot on beat 3 by hitting the tip of the stick on the drumhead while simultaneously hitting the shaft of the stick on the rim of the drum. This will take a little practice at first, but stick with it.

Finally, let's play the first measure of the two-bar fill with all the snare embellishments, continue on to the second measure with the sixteenth notes, rim shot, and simultaneous ride and kick hits, and with a little practice, you'll be playing the drum fill just like "Philly" Joe Jones plays it on the recording.

**Open Hi-Hat Foot Splash**

An *open hi-hat foot splash* is played by quickly bouncing the ball of the foot off the hi-hat pedal and raising the foot off of the pedal immediately after the cymbals have made contact with each other. The resulting sound is similar to playing a slightly open hi-hat with a drumstick and then letting the cymbals ring openly afterwards. When notated, an open hi-hat foot splash looks like this:

# "So What"
## FROM MILES DAVIS'S
## *KIND OF BLUE* (1959)

Jimmy Cobb's legendary drum fill from the opening track of the most famous jazz recording of all-time stands among the best drumming moments in history. Cobb, playing with a stick in his left hand and a wire brush in his right, effortlessly combines the snare, toms, kick, and open/closed hi-hat to create a gorgeous fill that launches Miles and the band into jazz bliss. Notice how Cobb, in all his glory, switches the wire brush over to his left hand and the stick to over his right hand after he hits the crash at the conclusion of the drum fill. Very cool stuff!

**Original transcription (1:29):**

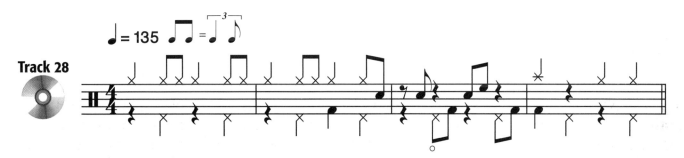

Let's start by playing and repeating a simplified version of the fill. Begin by hitting the crash cymbal with the stick in your left hand, and continue by playing a swing pattern on the ride with the brush in your right hand. Hit the kick drum on beat 3, and hit the snare drum with your right brush on the "&" of beat 4. Continue the fill by playing another snare hit with the right brush on the "&" of beat 1 of the following measure, and then an open hi-hat splash with your left foot on beat 2. Creating this open hi-hat splash sound with your foot will take some effort, but with a little practice, you'll be playing it in no time. This lesson concludes with another snare hit on beat 3 followed by a hi-hat hit with your left foot on beat 4, and then the whole exercise repeats. Go ahead and give it a try.

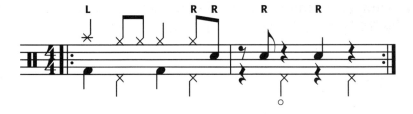

Now, let's try it again, but this time, we'll add an extra tom hit and a couple kick drum hits to the end of the fill.

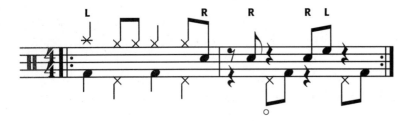

Finally, let's put it in context of the beat, and switch the wire brush to your left hand and the drumstick to your right hand immediately after hitting the crash on beat 1 at the end of the drum fill. This switch will take some practice, but be patient and stick with it!

 **Stick Shot**

*A stick shot* is played by placing the tip of one drumstick on the head of the snare drum while simultaneously hitting the shaft of the stick with the shaft of your other drumstick. The resulting sound is a loud, accented, woody crack.

When notated, a stick shot looks like this:

# "In Walked Bud" (ex. 3)
## FROM THELONIOUS MONK'S *THE VERY BEST* (2005, SONG ORIGINALLY RECORDED IN 1947)

Art Blakey plays a drag immediately followed by a stick shot in this short drum fill. Play the drag by softly bouncing your right stick on the snare drumhead twice and then hitting the head with the left stick once on beat 1. Press the left drumstick into the drumhead rather than letting it bounce freely off the head like you normally would, and strike the left drumstick with the right drumstick on the "&" of beat 1. Then hit the snare with a normal stroke on the "&" of beat 2, followed by slightly-open hi-hats and the kick drum simultaneously on beat 3, and continue by playing a basic swing pattern on the slightly-open hi-hats.

**Original transcription (2:12):**

Now, let's try playing the drum fill within the context of the song.

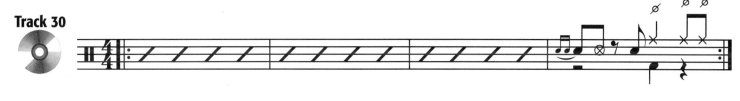

# "Chelsea Bridge"
## FROM BUDDY RICH'S *THE BEST OF BUDDY RICH (PACIFIC JAZZ)* (1997, SONG ORIGINALLY RECORDED IN 1970)

Buddy Rich plays some smooth, well-placed drum fills in this section of the tune. Listen to how nicely he incorporates a roll into the third measure of this excerpt.

**Original transcription (2:24):**

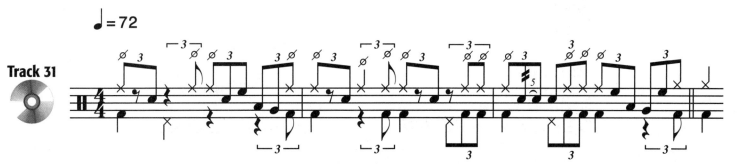

Let's start by isolating and repeating the first measure of this excerpt. Start slowly at first, and gradually increase the tempo as you feel comfortable.

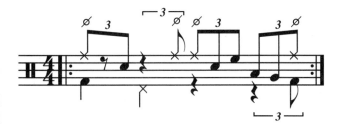

Next, let's isolate and repeat the second measure of the excerpt.

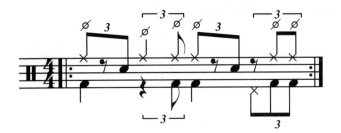

The fill incorporates a 5-stroke roll, which means the drum is struck five times throughout the course of the roll (RR–LL–R). The 5-stroke roll starts on the second note of the triplet that starts on beat 1 and ends on the last note of the triplet that starts on beat 1. Practice playing the 5-stroke roll within the beat by playing and repeating this exercise.

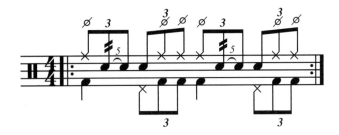

Now, let's isolate and repeat the entire third measure of the excerpt. Start slowly at first, and gradually increase the tempo as you feel comfortable.

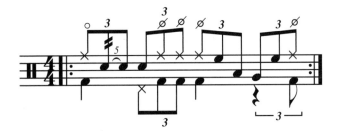

Finally, put it all together and play the fills just like Buddy Rich played them on the recording!

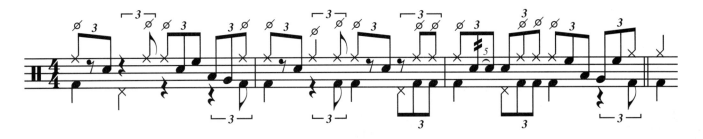

# "In Walked Bud" (ex. 4)
## FROM THELONIOUS MONK'S *THE VERY BEST* (2005, SONG ORIGINALLY RECORDED IN 1947)

Art Blakey incorporates a series of alternating stick shots and kick drum hits that are sandwiched in between a couple of drum rolls in this two-bar solo. Try playing the fill very slowly at first, and gradually increase the tempo as you feel comfortable.

**Original transcription (1:24):**

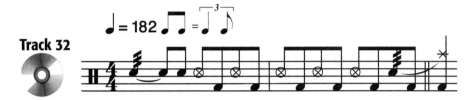

Track 32

### Trading Fours

*Trading fours* describes when a group of two or more musicians each take turns playing a four-measure solo.

### Buzz Strokes

A *buzz stroke* is a type of hit where the drumstick is pushed into the drumhead so it makes a buzzing sound. The buzz stroke essentially isolates what one drumstick plays in each stroke of a multiple bounce roll, also called a press roll or a buzz roll. When notated, a buzz stroke looks like this:

### Sextuplets

A *sextuplet* is a group of six notes played in the time of four notes of the same value. Sextuplets are identified by a small numeral 6 over the note group. When notated, sextuplets look like this:

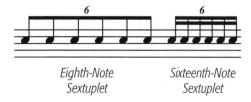

Eighth-Note
Sextuplet

Sixteenth-Note
Sextuplet

# "Blues Walk"
## FROM LOU DONALDSON'S *BLUES WALK* (1958)

In this excerpt, drummer Dave Bailey is trading fours with Ray Barretta on congas. This transcription focuses on Bailey's first three drum solos.

**Original transcription (3:58–4:35):**

Let's start by isolating and repeating the first measure of Bailey's first solo. Play a flam on beat 1, a buzz stroke on beat 3, and a stick shot on beat 4, all on the snare, while playing the kick on the "&" of beats 1 and 4 and on beat 2, and while playing the hi-hat with your foot on beat 3.

Now, let's isolate and repeat the second measure of the first solo.

Next, let's isolate and repeat the third measure of the first solo. Bailey plays with some fancy footwork and ends the measure with a buzz stroke on the snare on the "&" of beat 4.

Finally, let's isolate and repeat the fourth measure of the first solo and the first measure of the conga solo. Bailey begins the last measure of his first solo with a buzz stroke on the high rack tom, and continues with sixteenth notes on the snare. The slashes that you see on beats 3 and 4 indicate that the stick should be bounced while playing that sixteenth note, similar to a double stroke roll, but with the double stroke only in your right hand.

Finally, let's play the entire first drum solo.

Now, let's isolate and repeat the first measure of Bailey's second solo.

Next, let's isolate and repeat the second measure of the second solo.

Now, let's isolate and repeat the third measure of the second solo. This measure ends with a sextuplet that begins on beat 4.

Finally, let's isolate and repeat the fourth measure of the second solo and the first measure of the second conga solo. This section of the solo features three consecutive sextuplets starting on beat 2. End the run of sextuplets by simultaneously hitting the ride and the kick, and then play the hi-hat with your foot on beats 2 and 4 while Barretta plays his four-measure solo.

Finally, let's play the entire second drum solo.

Now, let's isolate and repeat the first two measures of the third drum solo.

Next, let's isolate and repeat the third measure of the third drum solo.

Now, let's focus on the last measure of the third drum solo, which contains a sextuplet on beat 3.

Finally, let's play the entire third drum solo.

# "Money"
## FROM PINK FLOYD'S *THE DARK SIDE OF THE MOON* (1973)

*The Dark Side of the Moon* is one of the most popular albums of all time. It was in the *Billboard* charts for an unprecedented 741 consecutive weeks and over 45 million copies of the album have been sold to date. Drummer Nick Mason plays along with Roger Waters's famous bass groove that is in $\frac{7}{4}$. That means there are seven beats to a measure, and the quarter note gets the count.

**Original transcription (0:26):**

Let's get comfortable with the $\frac{7}{4}$ time signature by playing this simplified version of Nick Mason's groove.

Add crash cymbal hits on beats 1 and 7, and an extra kick drum hit on the "ah" of beat 3, and you'll be playing the groove just like Nick Mason plays it on the recording!

# "I Never Loved A Man (The Way I Love You)"
## FROM ARETHA FRANKLIN'S *I NEVER LOVED A MAN THE WAY I LOVE YOU* (1967)

Drummer Gene Chrisman plays a wonderful groove in $\frac{3}{4}$ on this tune, sung by the Queen of Soul, Aretha Franklin, on her first single with Atlantic records. In this groove, there are three beats to each measure, and the quarter note gets the count.

**Original transcription (1:05):**

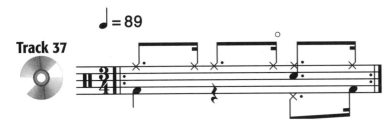

Let's start by playing a shuffle beat on the hi-hat, with hits on beats 1, 2, and 3, and on the "ah" of beats 1, 2, and 3. Also play the kick on beat 1, and the snare on beat 3. Go ahead and give it a try.

Next, let's play the same groove as in the previous exercise, but this time, we'll add another kick hit on the "ah" of beat 3.

Finally, play the same groove as in the previous exercise, but this time, raise your left foot off the hi-hat pedal on the "ah" of beat 2 and stomp it back down on the pedal on beat 3. Practice slowly at first and gradually increase the tempo as you feel comfortable.

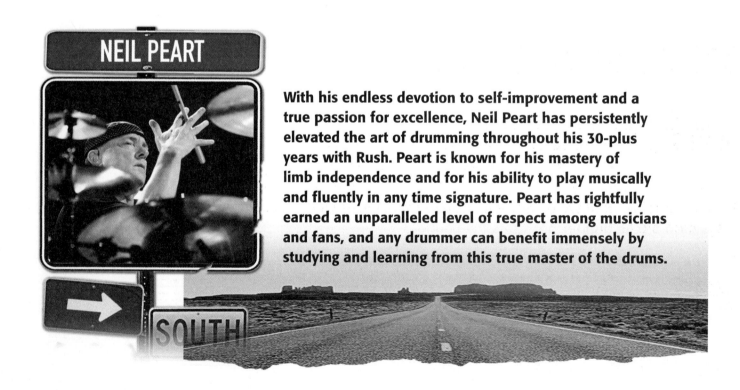

**NEIL PEART**

With his endless devotion to self-improvement and a true passion for excellence, Neil Peart has persistently elevated the art of drumming throughout his 30-plus years with Rush. Peart is known for his mastery of limb independence and for his ability to play musically and fluently in any time signature. Peart has rightfully earned an unparalleled level of respect among musicians and fans, and any drummer can benefit immensely by studying and learning from this true master of the drums.

# "The Trees"
## FROM RUSH'S *HEMISPHERES* (1978)

Neil Peart is one of the most respected and talented drummers to ever play the instrument, and he's inspired countless people to pick up the sticks and play the drums. Peart is revered for his ability to play well in any time signature. This excerpt and lesson features Neil Peart's $\frac{5}{4}$ groove on "The Trees."

**Original transcription (2:53):**

Let's start by playing quarter notes on the bell of the ride cymbal, the snare on beats 2 and 4, and the kick on beats 1 and 5.

Now, let's play the same groove as in the previous lesson, but this time, we'll add kick hits on the "&" of beats 2, 3, and 5.

Next, let's play quarter notes on the bell of the ride cymbal, the snare on beats 1, 2, and 4, and the kick on the "&" of beats 2 and 3, on beat 5, and on the "ah" of beat 5.

Finally, combine what we've learned in the previous lessons and play the $\frac{5}{4}$ groove just like Neil Peart plays it on the recording!

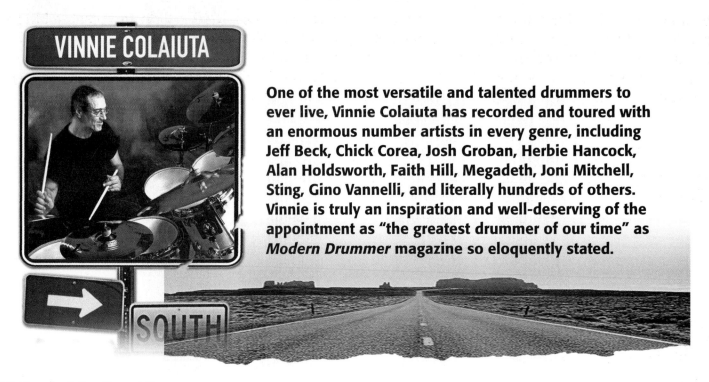

VINNIE COLAIUTA

One of the most versatile and talented drummers to ever live, Vinnie Colaiuta has recorded and toured with an enormous number artists in every genre, including Jeff Beck, Chick Corea, Josh Groban, Herbie Hancock, Alan Holdsworth, Faith Hill, Megadeth, Joni Mitchell, Sting, Gino Vannelli, and literally hundreds of others. Vinnie is truly an inspiration and well-deserving of the appointment as "the greatest drummer of our time" as *Modern Drummer* magazine so eloquently stated.

# "I Hung My Head"
## FROM STING'S *MERCURY FALLING* (1996)

Drummer Vinnie Colaiuta plays this 9/8 groove so it flows almost effortlessly with a steady accent on every other hi-hat hit. Few drummers have mastered both the technical wizardry and the musical depth of Vinnie Colaiuta. He is without a doubt one of the greatest drummers who has ever lived.

**Original transcription (2:20):**

Let's start by playing this simplified groove in 4/4.

Now, let's play the same beat, but this time we'll add one extra hi-hat hit at the end of the measure. You can count along with this as indicated on the example below.

Next, alternate each hi-hat hit between accented and unaccented notes, starting with an accented hit on beat 1. Notice that in the first measure, you are playing accents on all the odd-numbered beats (beats 1, 3, 5, 7, and 9) and on the second measure, you are playing on all the even numbered beats (beats 2, 4, 6, and 8). This is a clever trick that makes time signatures like this flow very effortlessly. Start very slowly and increase the tempo as you feel comfortable. With a little practice, you'll be playing the groove nice and easy.

# "Tom Sawyer"
## FROM RUSH'S *MOVING PICTURES* (1981)

This is one of Rush's most famous songs, and it's one of the most inspirational tunes the band has ever released. Neil Peart plays a very interesting groove in $\frac{7}{8}$ in this section of the tune that perfectly compliments Geddy Lee's synthesizer part.

**Original transcription (1:37):**

Track 40

Let's start by getting familiar with the $\frac{7}{8}$ time signature. There are seven beats to the measure, and the eighth note gets the count. Begin by playing sixteenth notes on the hi-hat with your right hand, the snare on beats 3 and 7, and the kick on beats 1, 2, and 6, and on the "&" of beat 4. It will take some practice to get used to playing in this time signature, so start slow, count out loud as you play, and gradually increase the tempo as you feel comfortable.

Now, let's play the same exact groove that we played in the previous lesson, but this time, we'll open the hi-hat on the "&" of beat 4 by lifting our foot off the hi-hat pedal, and stomping it back down again on beat 5. Go ahead and give it a try.

Next, let's play the same beat as in the previous exercise, except this time, well leave the hi-hat closed throughout and we'll move the kick hit from beat 6 to the "&" of beat 5.

Now, let's play the same exact groove that we played in the previous lesson, but this time, we'll open the hi-hat on the "&" of beats 4 and 5 by lifting our foot off the hi-hat pedal on the "&" of beat 4, stomping it back down again on beat 5, lifting it up again on the "&" of beat 5, and stomping it back down again on beat 6. Go ahead and give it a try.

Finally, let's put it all together and play the $\frac{7}{8}$ groove just like Neil Peart plays it on the recording!

### Double Time

A *double-time* groove is a type of groove that contracts one measure into half of a measure. The most common and simplest application of a double-time groove is achieved by moving the snare drum backbeat from beats 2 and 4, to the "&" of beats 1, 2, 3, and 4. Note values and tempos are not changed when switching between regular-time and double-time grooves; only the *feel* of the groove changes.

# "Me and Bobby McGee"
## FROM JANIS JOPLIN'S *PEARL* (1971)

Janis Joplin, one of the greatest singers of all time, recorded this tune just a few days before her death on October 4, 1970, and the album that hosted this classic was released just four months later. Drummer Clark Pierson gives the song a boost at three minutes into the track by shifting his drum beat from playing in regular time to playing in double time.

**Original transcription (2:56):**

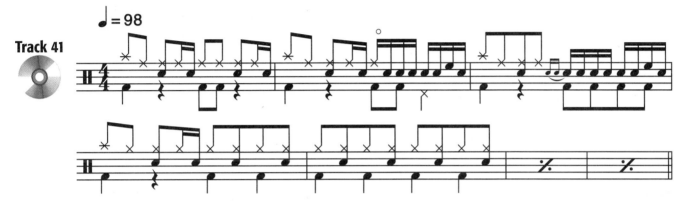

Let's begin with a simplified beat that will help us get comfortable with shifting from a regular-time groove to a double-time groove. In the first two measures, play eighth notes on the hi-hat, the kick on beats 1 and 3, and the snare on beats 2 and 4. Starting on measure three, play the kick on beats 1, 2, 3, and 4, and play the snare on the "&" of beats 1, 2, 3, and 4. Go ahead and give it a try.

Now, let's spice up the beat by adding a few crash hits, some extra hits on the snare and kick, and by switching from the hi-hat to the ride cymbal during the double-time section of this lesson. Start slowly and gradually increase the tempo as you feel comfortable.

Finally, add in a few more embellishments to make the beat authentic to what Clark Pierson played on the recording, and you'll be playing the groove just like it sounds on the album!

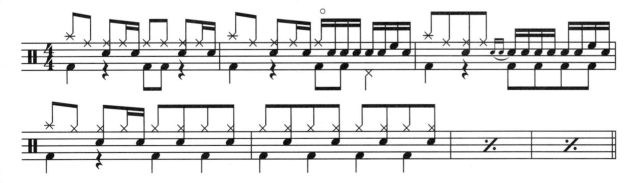

# "Wherever I May Roam"
## FROM METALLICA'S *METALLICA*, A.K.A. *THE BLACK ALBUM* (1991)

Powerhouse metal drummer Lars Ulrich shifts back and forth from regular time on the verses to half time on the choruses throughout this tune. We'll focus on one of these regular time to half time transitions in this excerpt and lesson.

### Half Time

A *half-time* groove is a type of groove that expands one measure into two measures. The most common and simplest application of a half-time groove is achieved by moving the snare drum backbeat from beats 2 and 4, to beat 3. Note values and tempos are not changed when switching between regular-time and half-time grooves; only the *feel* of the groove changes.

**Original transcription (2:10):**

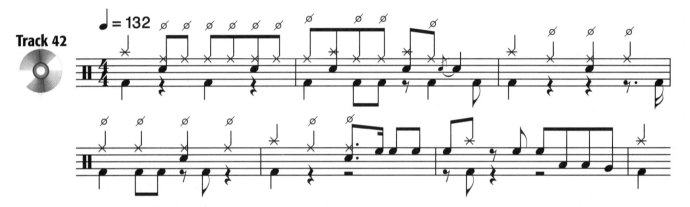

Let's begin by playing a simplified beat that starts in regular time and then transitions to half time. In the first two measures, play eighth notes on the hi-hat, the kick on beats 1 and 3, and the snare on beats 2 and 4. Starting on measure three, play quarter notes on the hi-hat, the kick on beat 1, and the snare on beat 3. Go ahead and give it a try!

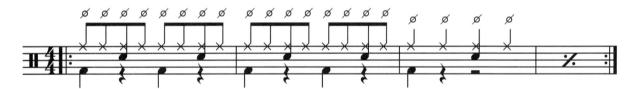

Now, let's add some extra transition notes on the snare and kick in measure two, and spice up the half-time section with an extra kick hit on the "ah" of beat 4.

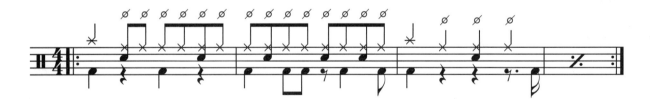

Finally, put it all together, and add some extra fills and embellishments as noted here. With a little practice, you'll be rocking this beat just like Lars Ulrich plays it on the recording!

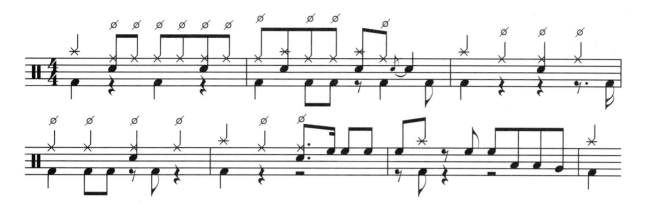

Metallica emerged in 1981, pioneering thrash metal in the United States at a time when glam was king, and they grew up to become metal's most famous and successful band. Lars Ulrich was firmly rooted behind the drumset, powering the band every step of the way. Lars has the ability to play hard and heavy whether he's playing his trademark lightening-fast double-kick thrash songs, or playing his slow epic grooves.

### Ritardando

*Ritardando* is a musical term used to indicate that the tempo is gradually slowing down.

### Accelerando

*Accelerando* is a musical term used to indicate that the tempo is gradually speeding up.

# "Stand"
## FROM BLUES TRAVELER'S *FOUR* (1994)

Drummer Brendan Hill guides the band through all sorts of tempo / time / meter manipulations on this tune. He switches from regular time to half time while giving the tempo a slight ritardando during his drum fill at 2:17 before leading the band through a very slow and steady accelerando over the next two minutes of the tune.

**Track 43**  **Original transcription (2:10):**

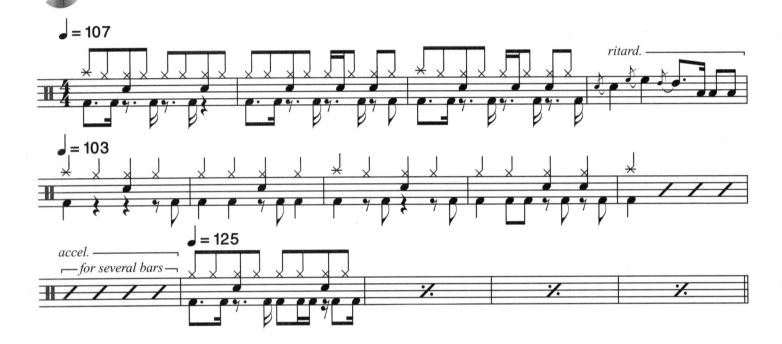

Let's start by playing a measure of regular-time at ♩ = 107 BPM, followed by the dramatic fill that ritardandos into a half-time groove at ♩ = 103 BPM.

Now, let's practice transitioning from a slow half-time groove at ♩ = 103 BPM that accelerandos to a regular-time groove at ♩ = 125 BPM.

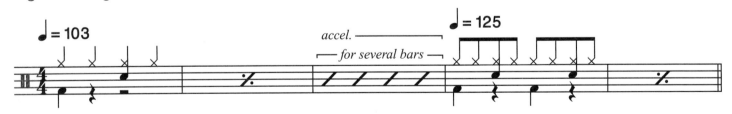

Finally, add in all the embellishments to make it sound like the recording, and really drag out the accelerando so it occurs over roughly two minutes of playing. Try making the tempo accelerate in a very steady, evenly paced manner.

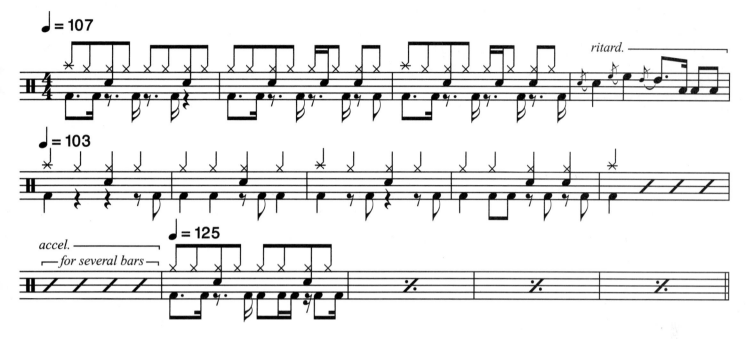

# Congratulations!

You have completed **Level 3** of the
*On the Beaten Path: Beginning Drumset Course.* **You now have
all the tools you need** to play a
variety of **musical styles,**

and to start working through
the other **On the Beaten Path**
series of books, like

*On the Beaten Path: The Drummer's Guide to Musical Styles
and the Legends Who Defined Them, On the Beaten Path: Metal,* **and**
*On the Beaten Path: Jazz,*

to name a few. **And please,** if you're not already
playing in a **band**, it's time to find some musicians
to start playing with!
There's no greater feeling than **playing the drums**
and the music you love, so keep on drumming
**On the Beaten Path!**